"*Seduce Me!* is such a quick read. I couldn't wait to get to each new chapter. If you love your partner, read this book! "

    - Dorrie E.

"Finally, a book that helps me understand women! A must read for all men who want better sex."

    - Don A.

"Where was this book 10 years ago? Every man and woman needs to read it. Especially a certain ex of mine!"

    - Pat S.

"The seduction stories seduced my thoughts, my feelings, and my body. Now it's my boyfriend's turn!"

    - Tiffany G.

"This book is excellent! The process is simple, yet really hits the mark. I've thoroughly enjoyed it."

    - Michele D.

To the love of my life – this book's inspiration – and to my cherished family.
Thank you for your love, support, and talents, without which nothing could be accomplished.

TABLE OF CONTENTS

Introduction

All across America there has been a renewed commitment to long-term relationships. Understanding that 50% of marriages will end in divorce, more and more couples are seeking professional counseling and training to learn the skills necessary to keep their relationships intact.

Yet, many are dissatisfied with the sexual component of their relationships. The National Health and Social Life Survey determined that 43% of women and 31% of men have some type of sexual dysfunction. Moreover, experts estimate that over 40 million women have lost their desire for sex!

What is happening with these relationships? Why do so many committed couples struggle with such an essential and pleasurable part of their relationship?

It turns out that in addition to psychological and sociological factors, our biochemistry plays a role. A great deal has been written to help couples understand relationships from a psychological point of view, but not as much about the biological forces that significantly impact our sexual arousal processes. Scientists have discovered that certain biochemicals increase our desire for sex and others decrease it. And while researchers are discovering more every day, not enough of what scientists have already determined -- and how couples can apply this research -- has been broadly disseminated to the general public. Until now.

Hormones and neurotransmitters affect the way we think, act and feel. We're all familiar with adrenaline, which surges in response to threatening situations. For instance, if we suddenly perceive danger, adrenaline is released as our fight or flight response system kicks in, causing our hearts to beat faster and our blood pressure to rise. We start taking short quick breaths and our senses become more acute as our bodies prepare for rapid response.

People pumped with adrenaline have been known to perform superhuman acts. Eventually, the threat of danger disappears and our bodies return to normal. The initiation of the adrenaline process is not a conscious one. We don't tell ourselves to release more adrenaline in order to respond with fight or flight. In the face of danger, our bodies go on a form of autopilot in order to prime ourselves for optimal response.

This is an example of how our bodies perceive external stimuli and respond with biochemical changes that affect the way we perform. Several other biochemical reactions take place in our bodies in response to external or internal stimuli. *Seduce Me!* explores those that specifically affect sexual arousal, both positively and negatively.

In addition to helping us understand the role of biochemical and psychological factors in our libidos, *Seduce Me!* presents methods that can reactivate the body's sexual arousal systems. You can learn how to ignite – or re-ignite – your partner's passion and regularly experience ultimate sexual pleasure.

- ***Seduce Me!*** is for couples who have lost the spark they once had and want to get it back.

- ***Seduce Me!*** is for couples who never fully developed their sexual selves and are ready to learn.

- *Seduce Me!* is for couples who are currently having sensational sex, and want to make sure it will continue.

Seduce Me! demonstrates that sensational sex does not require having sex 5 times a day, having multiple simultaneous orgasms, or having 60 minutes of intercourse. It doesn't require model-perfect looks or body-builder muscles and you certainly don't have to be young. It doesn't even require partners that are experts on the latest techniques. All it takes is a true desire to understand your partner's needs and a willingness to explore ways of meeting them.

Inside every man is a potential Don Juan and in every women, the passion of Lady Chatterley. Unfortunately, he's often too busy being "Mr. Hardworking-breadwinner-without-enough-time-for-family," while she's trying to balance Murphy Brown, June Cleaver, and Martha Stewart.

But even in our hectic, complicated, and overwhelming work and family lives, there is room for passion and intimacy. In fact, passion and intimacy can help keep our relationships strong enough to handle the day-to-day chaos.

Darcy A. Cole

Most of us have had passionate sex at least once in our lives. If you had it before and now don't – you can get it back...if you've never had it, you will soon!

> *If sex is such a natural phenomenon, how come there are so many books on how to do it?*
>
> -- Bette Midler

CHAPTER ONE

1. What Happened?

> We used to have sex in the house, outside the house, in the car, in the park. You name it, we explored it. It didn't take hours of foreplay to get Marcia ready for me. Now, I have to work hard at getting her interested in sex, and sometimes no matter what I do, she still doesn't want it.
>
> John, age 28

Remember in the beginning of your relationship when you couldn't keep your hands off each other? When you could hardly concentrate on anything because your mind was always on your partner? When all you had to do was think about your partner and you became aroused?

Seduce Me!

How often do we hear, "Before, I didn't have to work to get her in the mood. She wanted sex as much as I did! *I* still do, but she's changed"?

What happened? Where did the passion go?

Many couples worry that they're no longer attracted to one another and begin to fear that the relationship is in trouble. What isn't well known, however, is that there is a scientific explanation for some of these changes and there may not be anything at all wrong with their relationships.

Our body's chemistry changes during the course of a love relationship and it is these chemical changes that dramatically affect our desire for sex. When we're in the initial, or *infatuation*, stage of a relationship, several chemicals are coursing throughout our bodies changing the way we think, act, and feel. Scientists have discovered that during infatuation, our bodies increase production of dopamine, norepinephrine, and phenylethylamine (PEA). These natural chemicals combine to cause us to feel what scientists call a "love high." In addition to increasing our desire for sex, they cause our bodies to have

- Racing hearts, dilated pupils and sweaty palms

Darcy A. Cole

- Feelings of euphoria

- Obsessive feelings towards our partner

- Decreased hunger

- Problems sleeping

- Blindness to our partner's flaws

Sound familiar? Remember staying up all night on the phone with your new love trying to talk each other into being the first one to hang up the phone? *"No, you hang up first."* It wasn't that you'd both suddenly become the most brilliant chatters on earth that kept you on the phone all night, it was these infatuation chemicals that caused you to feel a love high whenever you connected with your new partner.

We've all witnessed the powerful effects of infatuation on our friends as well. I recall the reaction of one of my friends, who was "madly in love" with her new boyfriend, to his gift to her of a new Harley Davidson toilet seat cover. "Isn't that the sweetest present?" she gushed dreamily. Hmmm, sounds suspiciously like the work of certain infatuation chemicals.

Seduce Me!

16

Falling in love is such a wonderful feeling: from the ever-present smiles on our faces to the instant arousal whenever we think of our new partners. We fondly remember the passionate sex of the beginning, but we forget how much time we spent thinking and daydreaming about our new loves. In fact, romantic love triggers in us similar biochemistry to that of people with *obsessive-compulsive disorder*, according to Dr. Helen E. Fisher of Rutgers University. Her research (as cited in Barclay, 2001) reveals that this biochemistry results in some of us spending up to 85% of our waking hours thinking about our new partners!

No wonder we could hardly get anything else done during that stage!

Eventually we move out of the infatuation stage to the enduring love stage. This takes place usually between six months and three years into our relationships, along with a decrease in the chemicals that caused us to feel powerful love highs and instant sexual desire for one another.

At this stage, different chemicals take over and our love becomes deeper and richer. We nurture each other and develop a comfortable attachment. In this stage, we become more intimate, sharing our true selves. Our hormones don't

Darcy A. Cole

drive our passionate sex as much as our feelings of connectedness (Liebowitz, 1983).

> *We just celebrated our 9th anniversary and we spent it at a nice hotel in the city. It wasn't the same intensity as it used to be, but our lovemaking was very good. He knows me and my body so well now. Sometimes I miss the 'can't-wait-to-rip-your-clothes-off' feeling, but I like what we have now also.*
>
> Susan, age 37

In addition to the drop in the infatuation chemicals, several other biological changes begin to interfere with our sex drives. In her remarkable book, *The Alchemy of Love and Lust* (1996), Dr. Crenshaw discusses several of the hormones that affect our libidos. She helps us understand that various chemicals have significant effects on our desire for and enjoyment of sex. Some affect men more than women and vice versa, and some *increase* our desire while others *decrease* our desire.

One culprit is the hormone prolactin, which is known to decrease desire for sex among both men and women. Many couples report a sharp decline in their sex lives after having children and prolactin may be a primary reason. During pregnancy and nursing, prolactin increases considerably, as much as 10 times the normal level!

Another major sex drive destroyer is the hormone progesterone. Progesterone inhibits our desire for - and enjoyment of - sex (Meston & Frohlich 2000, Crenshaw 1996). Progesterone levels fluctuate during a woman's menstrual cycle and pregnancy. Its synthetic form is the primary ingredient of Depo Provera, Norplant, and several oral contraceptives, and is given during hormone replacement therapy in menopause.

Progesterone has such a negative impact on our sex drives that it has been dispensed to criminals as a form of chemical castration! How many women are deeply troubled by their lack of sexual desire and wonder what's wrong, when the cause might easily be the negative effects of their choice of birth control?

Stress is another factor that causes changes in our libidos. Remember that prolactin, which increases during pregnancy and nursing, has a strong negative impact on our desire for sex. Prolactin also increases during times of

---

psychological stress, and is so effective in reducing our libidos, it can even cause impotence.

Stress also lowers our levels of dehydroepiandrosterone (DHEA) and testosterone. Because these are two hormones that *increase* our sex drive, stress has a twofold negative impact by increasing a hormone that lowers our sexual desire, while lowering the level of two hormones that increase our sex drive.

> *I don't know what's wrong with me, but I'm never in the mood anymore. For years, I loved having sex with my husband, but ever since my 2-year-old daughter was born, I just haven't been able to get excited for sex. I keep telling him it's not him, but I don't really know what it is. He's lucky if we have sex once a month. I love my husband very much and I can't imagine my life without him. I'm so afraid he's going to leave me for someone else. I worry about it constantly. I know he's frustrated with me and I'm running out of excuses.*
>
> Linda, age 31

Seduce Me!

Linda doesn't realize that her worrying about not meeting her husband's sexual needs is actually exacerbating the problem. The more she worries and stresses about him leaving, she is provoking changes in her hormones that lower her sex drive even further.

It's no wonder that couples start wondering what happened. Birth control, financial worries, work stress, illness, childbirth, and relationship problems all affect certain hormones in our bodies that decrease our desire for sex.

Men and women think something is wrong with the relationship because they don't feel the same instant arousal as they did before. But as you can see, it may just be a matter of biochemistry.

Regardless of the causes, however, it doesn't mean that the passion in long-term relationships has to end. In fact, as you will soon learn, sex can be better than before and as passionate as ever.

Darcy A. Cole

2. Sex, How Important Is It Anyway?

> *My boyfriend wants us to have sex at least once or twice a day. I could easily get by with once a week or even less. Don't get me wrong, our sex is good. It's just that he thinks there is something wrong with us because we're not having sex every day. I'm tired of fighting with him about it. There are more important things than sex.*
>
> Carla, age 27

On average, American couples have sex about once a week, however, there is a wide variance. Some couples have sex every day and others only a few times a year. Many couples disagree about the level of importance sex should have in a

---

Seduce Me!

relationship. This is especially true after the infatuation period ends and arousal isn't as easy as it was before.

So how important is it? It depends on whom you ask, the partner who is happy with the couple's sex or the one who isn't!

Experts tell us that sex shouldn't be the essence of a relationship, but it is a physical expression of the relationship. Making love can be very beneficial to relationships by helping couples

- Strengthen intimacy

- Communicate desire and attraction

- Express love for one another

- Bring pleasure to one another

- Learn about each other's needs and wants

- Relieve stress

- Experience mutual delight

- Communicate needs

Darcy A. Cole

- Discover new pleasures together

Furthermore, scientists have found that sex causes several chemical changes in our bodies that are helpful to our health and well-being. Sexual activity increases our bodies' production of endorphins and oxytocin, two chemicals that have profound effects on our bodies.

Endorphins are the body's natural painkiller. When they were first discovered in the late 1970s, they were named "endorphins", from the two words "endogenous" and "morphine" because they mimic the positive effects of morphine, but are produced naturally in our own bodies.

During sex, endorphin production increases by as much as 200%!

In addition to relieving pain, endorphins are the cause of that euphoric feeling after sex. They have been shown to

- Reduce stress

- Improve our immune systems

- Heal tissues

- Create a sense of well-being

Seduce Me!

(There goes that "I have a headache" excuse!)

Oxytocin is another natural substance our bodies benefit from during sex. Called the "touch hormone", it is released throughout our bodies when we experience touch, genital stimulation, and orgasm.

Oxytocin creates in us a sense of attachment to the person who is touching us. It also creates in us a desire to be touched even more.

Orgasm causes oxytocin levels to increase three to five times the normal level. The more we are touched, the more our levels of oxytocin increase, which increases bonding with our partners and a desire to be touched even more. *It's a beautiful thing!*

Furthermore, sex benefits us as we get older by slowing down the aging process of certain physiological systems (Crenshaw, 1996).

Clearly, sex can provide several individual physical and emotional advantages as well as help us nourish the intimacy of our relationships.

Darcy A. Cole

> Want to look 10 years younger?
>
> *Have more sex! In his decade long study, Dr. David Weeks, a neuropsychologist at the Royal Edinburgh Hospital found that people who have sex 3 or more times a week look more than 10 years younger than the average person* (BBC, 1999).

The majority of Americans believe that an active sex life is essential to their happiness. This continues to be true even as people get older according to the American Association of Retired Persons (AARP, 1999), who found that 67% of men and 57% of women say that a satisfying sexual relationship is important to the quality of life.

Unfortunately, many couples aren't satisfied with either the quality or the quantity of their sex lives. The National Health and Social Life Survey (CNN, 1999) found that 43% of women and 31% of men age 18 – 59 experience sexual dysfunction.

For women, the biggest problem is lack of desire. Dr. Hilda Hutcherson, author of *What our Mother's Never Told Us About Sex*, says that one-third of women are not interested in sex and of those having sex, one-half aren't satisfied (*Oprah* June 12, 1999).

> *I have to admit it, I feel like I'm in a prison. My wife just doesn't want to have sex any more. We've only had sex 3 times in the last 5 months. When I try to talk to her about it, she just says she's too tired for sex. I've tried being understanding, being romantic, doing more chores around the house. I don't know what else to do. I have plenty of opportunities to get it somewhere else, but I don't want other women, I want her. I love her and my sons and except for this, we have a great marriage. If it's like this now, when we're still young and healthy, what will it be like in 20 years? How long can we survive?*
>
> Phillip, age 33

Can a relationship survive without sex?

It depends on one's definition of "survive." Couples can survive forever without even being in the same room! But what about thriving? Can a couple have a healthy satisfying relationship without sex? Only as long as *both* partners are happy without it, which isn't often the case.

Darcy A. Cole

Talk show host and author Dr. Phil McGraw says, however, "Sexless marriages are an undeniable epidemic in America" and because "sex and intimacy are a meaningful part of a relationship, loss of sexual desire can severely affect a marriage."

If one or more partners are dissatisfied with either the quality or quantity of sex, then it can lead to serious problems. And in spite of our best facades, ignoring or pretending that there isn't a disconnect won't make it go away. Like any ignored problem, it festers and creates resentment that can poison an otherwise good relationship.

If you're in a relationship that has a sexual disconnect, it is vital that both partners work on resolving the differences.

It is clear that sex has profound effects on a relationship. If it's good, the benefits to the individuals as well as the relationship are significant. If it's not, then the relationship may experience problems.

The good news is that couples don't have to suffer because of sexual difficulties.

Couples can have sensational sex for as long as they want - and as often as they want! As many as 25% of couples over the age of 75 report that they have sex an average of once per week! Moreover, sexually active couples over 75 say sex gets even better with age (Starr & Weiner, 1982)! Who said aging doesn't have its benefits?

> Recently, Asian researchers found that more sex will improve the economy!
>
> *SINGAPORE, NOV. 12, 2002 (CBS News) - If people have more sex, they will be happier and more motivated to work and, consequently, the economy will improve, Asian sexologists said at a conference Thursday while calling for more sexual education across the continent.*
>
> (Does this mean it's our patriotic duty?)

Darcy A. Cole

CHAPTER THREE

3. Getting your Partner Ready

The Perfect Evening

A husband and wife go bowling and decide to make a bet on the outcome of their games, with the winner getting the reward of his or her choice.

The wife says, "If I win, I want you to fill the bedroom with lit scented candles and have romantic music playing in the background. I want you to give me a bouquet of fresh flowers with a poem that you wrote ahead of time telling me why you love me.

"Then after dancing with me for hours, I want you to carry me to the bed and slowly remove my

---

Seduce Me!

> *clothes. Then I want you to tell me how beautiful you think I am and give me soft kisses all over my body."*
>
> *Satisfied that she had described the perfect evening, she then asks him what he wants if he wins. He thinks for a second, and then says "a blow job."*

When it comes to sex and desire, there are significant differences between men and women. Some of these differences are biological and some are sociological.

Arousal Differences between Men and Women

We know what happens to most men physically when they see a naked woman – even if it's only a picture in *Playboy* or in a movie. It usually doesn't take much more than a sexy visual to start the arousal process.

But while men are very visually responsive, looking at pictures of naked men doesn't do anything for most women …that's right - nothing, nada, zip, not a thing!

Sure, they may stare at *Playgirl's* centerfold (mostly out of curiosity), but as far as turning them on…forget about it (except maybe when they're in the infatuation stage). It isn't

Darcy A. Cole

that men aren't attractive or sexy to women, it's just that they don't get aroused by visuals the same way that guys do. So the next time she barely notices as you prance around in nothing but your bath towel, don't take it personally if she isn't in a hurry to take it off you. She's just not programmed to get physically aroused by seeing your naked bod.

I know many guys find this disappointing, but it is what it is.

A second major difference between men and women is that a man can get turned on with nothing more than physical stimulation. That is, if a man is completely *un*aroused and a woman starts rubbing his penis through his pants, there can be an immediate physical response indicating his arousal.

This is often not true for women, however. If you start rubbing any of her sex parts before she's ready, then you might as well call it a night. It can be a complete turn-off.

Even she appears to be getting aroused physically, it does not mean that she is getting turned on. In fact, sex researchers consider the female arousal system as having two forms: *Physiological* arousal, indicated by her body's measurable response, (i.e., vaginal lubrication, increased blood flow to the vulva) and *subjective* arousal when a woman self-reports that she is turned-on and sexually excited (Meston & Frohlich, 2000).

It is important not to confuse her *body's* indication of arousal with her desire for sex. A woman can have physical symptoms of being aroused during certain occasions when she is not interested in, or desirous of, sex at all.

For example, if she becomes lubricated during her gynecological exam, if her nipples get hard in cold weather, or in response to breastfeeding, these physical effects do not indicate a desire for sex. In none of these situations is she sexually excited although her body is responding in a similar manner to when she is sexually aroused.

Sometimes she can become subjectively aroused as a result of being physiologically aroused, but often not.

It is completely reasonable that one would think that in order to turn a woman on he should start touching her body, because that is what works to get his body excited. But what works for men to get aroused does not typically work for women. In fact, touching a women's breasts, nipples, or

---

Darcy A. Cole

vagina before she is ready can actually create a negative physical reaction – an *anti*-arousal sensation.

Let's put it this way. Imagine that your left arm is itching because of a giant mosquito bite. Imagine how good it feels to vigorously scratch the bite…aah relief…the sharper the nails, the better they feel scratching your arm. Now imagine how it would feel if you scratched the right arm just as hard – except on this arm you don't have a mosquito bite. The scratching sensation on the right arm is unpleasant. The sharper the nails, the more it hurts. In order for you to enjoy the scratching on the right arm, you would have first needed a mosquito bite to create the itch.

This is a small example of how it can be for a woman if you touch her before she's ready. For your touch to feel good, she needs to be turned on first. If she isn't emotionally aroused first, your touching her can be as unpleasant as the feeling from scratching the arm without the itch of a mosquito bite.

Let's take this one step further. Imagine that you have the mosquito bite, but you're in a unique situation that prevents you from scratching it for 5 minutes (i.e., you're carrying furniture and can't put it down). Imagine your arm itching and itching and that you're getting almost desperate to get a chance to scratch it. Now imagine that whatever was preventing you from scratching it has finally ended and you can now scratch it. Oooh, imagine how good that feels – what a great relief (almost orgasmic really!) That scratching feels even better.

So what does this mean? This is critical. To seduce a woman, you have to be her "mosquito bite" first; you have to make her want your touch so bad that she's aching for relief.

This point cannot be emphasized enough. Before you start touching her, she has to want it. And the more she wants it, the better it will feel when you do touch her. You have to make her hungry for you.

How do you get her there?

The answer is: You have to seduce her mind in order to seduce her body. This is the key to female sexual desire.

- If you want to get her hungry for your touch

- If you want her to want sex as much as you want sex

Darcy A. Cole

- If you want her to fantasize about you when you're not together

- If you want to give her the ultimate physical pleasure

- If you want to feel like the most desirable man in the world

- If you want to find the passion you once had or create it for the first time

... then you have to seduce her mind first.

Seduce Her Mind and the Rest Will Follow

When thinking about the way to entice a woman, I'm reminded of the phrase, "Free your mind and the rest will follow." If we change this line to "Seduce her mind and the rest will follow," you then have the most effective strategy for igniting a woman's passion.

Seduce her mind and the rest will follow. Repeat it; memorize it; make it your new mantra, and don't forget it.

_____

Seduce Me!

You can think of seducing her mind as *mental foreplay*. Remember that several chemicals increase and decrease our desire for sex. Mental foreplay means engaging in activities that cause chemical changes that increase desire for sex.

It includes activities that cause changes in the hormones that are directly related to our libidos (PEA, DHEA, testosterone, dopamine, oxytocin) as discussed in Chapter 1. Many of these activities have long been known to increase sexual desire, but now we have the benefit of scientific research that helps explain how and why these activities cause men and women to become aroused.

For instance, scientists now believe that sexual emotions, fantasies, and images can raise hormones that boost sexual desire. Similarly, romantic memories, thoughts, and stories can provoke changes in chemicals that increase desire for sex (Barclay, 2001; Crenshaw, 1996; Liebowitz, 1983; Spink, 1996).

As you will soon learn, the *Seduce Me!* process for igniting your partner's desire includes activities that inspire sexual emotions, fantasies, images as well as romantic memories, thoughts and stories that effectively stimulate passionate sexual desire.

Darcy A. Cole

But before you can arouse her sexual brain, you have to overcome a few barriers.

Overcoming Obstacles

There are several mental obstacles that clutter the pathway and prevent her mind from being open to your seductive techniques.

Mental obstacles are not the same as *turn-offs*. A turn-off, for instance, might be watching TV during sex (we'll get to more of those later). Turn-offs can take place after already being sexually excited, whereas mental obstacles prevent us from even getting in the mood in the first place.

Several of these mental obstacles apply to men as well as women. Stress, performance anxiety, illnesses, hormonal deficiencies are just a few of them. Generally though, the female libido is more affected by mental obstacles than the male libido.

One reason for this is testosterone, which increases the desire for genital sex and orgasm. It is testosterone that enables men to become sexually aroused without the need for them to be "in the mood" first. Men naturally have as much as 40 times the amount of testosterone that women have. It is also the reason why men usually take a more aggressive role in pursuing sex rather than the receptive role that women take (Crenshaw, 1996).

Many women aren't even aware of these mental obstacles and how they impact their ability to feel sexual.

For instance, you may hear her say that she's too tired for sex. But a feeling of exhaustion can be the result of emotional, mental, or physical labor. And without analysis, she may not have any idea why she's just not in the mood.

A few of the most common mental obstacles are detailed here.

1. Brain Overload

Often women take on the role of being the *family manager*. We already know that having children decreases the female libido because of the changes in prolactin and progesterone. But what we're talking about here is the responsibility of taking care of the home and family, regardless of whether she also works outside the house or not.

As family managers, we feel tremendous pressure to make sure everything important gets done and, if we're lucky, goes smoothly. We feel that if we let down our guard, we will forget something and we will have let our families down. We define our success as wives and mothers with our ability to keep on top of everything related to each member of the immediate family.

In order to do this, we have a constant evolving "to-do" list running in our thoughts. This *mental checklist* is a list of dozens of things that need to be done and it is always on our minds.

If we're concentrating intently on something and our mind is focused on the task at hand, then our mental checklist is like the background music in an elevator. If we're not absorbed by something else, then our mental checklist is more like a live concert, in our face and loud. In any case, it is always there and we're constantly adding to it and crossing off completed tasks.

A small peek at one women's checklist might look like this:

Wake the kids up at 7:00. Make sure there is breakfast available; Nina ate the last of her favorite cereal yesterday. Scott has a field trip today; he needs to pack his lunch. Did I sign his permission slip? Remind him to take his allergy medicine; do I need to get a refill at the drug store yet? Oh yeah, I have to stop at the store anyway to pick up a birthday card for my sister and get it in the mail. How is my stamp supply? That reminds me, I need to remind John to call his mother tomorrow and wish her happy birthday. Oh no that won't work, we're supposed to go to Nina's recital tomorrow, John will have to call his mom tonight. And I really should call my friend Sandra tonight to give her support because she just broke up with her boyfriend. I'll get a card for her too while I'm at the store. Is there anything else I need to pick up while I'm at the store? How's the milk supply? Do I need to get anything for dinner for the rest of the week? I saw that they're having a special on chicken leg; I'll stock up. Is there any room left in the freezer? No, I have to clean it out. Speaking of cleaning, this house is a mess.

Darcy A. Cole

And on and on and on and on it goes.

Regular items on this list also include: laundry, homework, doctor and dentist appointments, banking, paying bills, house repairs, appliance maintenance, pet care, school projects and supplies, getting and sorting the mail, housework, communication tasks, etc.

It is truly an amazing amount of responsibility. Even if we can delegate some or most of it, it is still our responsibility to remember it, delegate it, and follow up on it. On top of this, most women work outside the home and they have all those responsibilities as well.

The point is that this mental to-do list keeps our minds fully occupied. It only takes a few times of forgetting to do something that causes us to make sure we keep this mental list running at all times. We're so afraid that if we give it a rest, we'll forget something important and we'll have abdicated our responsibilities *("then what kind of mother/wife would I be?")*. This creates anxiety that leaves little room for romance.

Implications. In order for a woman to fit romance into her schedule, we need to "free her mind". You can help her in several ways.

- ***Share the mental burden*:** First, ask her to list for you all of the things on her mental checklist. At this time, you have only one job and that is to listen to her tell you everything she believes needs to be done. At this point, you should not try to solve any of the problems on the list. Do not offer advice or question the validity of her list by saying something like, "Oh that's not really important; we don't have to do that." You are only to let her mind release by listening to her while she "shares the burden" with you.

  It would be good for you to write the items down as she tells you them as long as you are not making any comments about them. After she's done, validate the extensiveness of the list and the enormous responsibility she feels.

- ***Write out a to-do list*:** If you didn't write down all of the items on her mental checklist when she was telling you them, encourage her to write each item down to form a to-do list, either with you or not, so

Darcy A. Cole

that she can be relieved of having to constantly remember everything.

- *Relieve her of some responsibilities and chores:* Here is where you can together review the list and discuss the priorities. With her cooperation, agree to take over complete responsibility for some things on the list so she doesn't have to even think about them. Taking complete responsibility does not mean just letting her delegate the task to you. It means you now *own* full responsibility for getting it done and she should no longer even have it on her list.

- *Decrease the pressure:* She may be putting too much pressure on herself to be perfect and if that is the case, you can help her lower her expectations. You would rather have some relaxed time with her than to have all of the laundry caught up, for instance. Help her re-define her definition of a successful wife and mother to include self-care and happiness as opposed to making sure that the kitchen is spotless.

2. *Emotional Fatigue*

In addition to being the family manager, she is typically the family nurturer; responsible for meeting the emotional needs of her children, her husband, and her extended family. And she often overlooks her own needs to do so. She often defines success as a wife/mother by meeting everyone else's needs, even at the expense of her own.

For those of us with this responsibility, we know that our work never ends. We know that we never finish everything. We know that there is always more to do and that we will never "get off duty."

Typically, when you have a job outside of the house, at some point you are no longer "on duty." You are free to do something else. You are free to think about something else. But when you are responsible for the family and household, you are never off duty.

She knows that at any time and no matter what she's doing, she can be interrupted with a family matter. This can be anything from a call from her aunt needing help getting to the doctor, her children needing help resolving a loud fight, or her husband needing to find his favorite shirt. The issue can be minor or serious, but it always seems to be

Darcy A. Cole

urgent and a woman feels obligated to be at the beck and call of whoever needs her at a given moment.

She is often torn between conflicting needs. For instance if she has an outside job, she feels guilty about not being home when the kids get home from school. If she takes off work to be with a sick child, she feels guilty for not meeting her work responsibilities.

This affects her ability to get sexual in a number of ways. First, she cannot fully relax because she knows that at any moment her children could interrupt and she has to be prepared to help them.

Second, she spends the bulk of her emotional energy giving to her family and friends (and often co-workers) and she may see sex as just another method (or burden) of nurturing someone else – namely you. Remember that in order for her to get sexually excited, she needs to be emotionally seduced and frankly she's emotionally bankrupt because she's focused on nurturing everyone but herself.

Often she runs herself ragged and doesn't slow down until she becomes physically sick, and even then she feels guilty. When she says that she is too tired for sex, the

Seduce Me!

question isn't whether that's true or not. The question is whether it is physical, mental, or emotional exhaustion that is wearing her down.

Implications. In order to get romantic, she needs to be emotionally rejuvenated. She needs to learn how to get her needs met to give her the emotional strength and energy to be the family nurturer and manager. She needs to understand that it is in her family's best interest to take care of her emotional and physical needs, for the same reason that airplane personnel instruct us in the event of an emergency to put oxygen masks on ourselves before putting them on our children.

She needs to have time away from the house, without interruptions, and with full confidence that the kids will be taken care of while she's gone. Finally, she needs to feel that sex is something that is a gift for her and you – not just another thing she has to do for someone else. One way to help her with this is through *date night*, which we discuss in detail in the next chapter.

3. Body Image

A woman has to feel sexy in order to want sex. She not only has to believe that you find her attractive but also that she finds herself attractive. In fact, a recent study among overweight women (Areton, 2002) found that body image was the second most important indicator of sexual satisfaction (sexual communication was the highest predictor).

There is so much documentation about the societal pressures women face to look good. For her self-esteem to be directly related to her outward appearance is a sad but real fact in today's society. She is constantly bombarded with images of gorgeous models on TV, magazines, and in movies.

Guys, imagine if a large part of your self-esteem was dependent upon you being a millionaire, and the only men you saw in magazines, TV and in movies were millionaires. How would you feel if you saw that women were only attracted to millionaires, and anyone making less than $300,000 a year was considered unacceptable and even the brunt of put down jokes.

Seduce Me!

It would be ridiculous considering the U.S. Department of Labor calculates the average American salary to be in the $30,000 range (2002). Then how ridiculous is it to compare the average American woman, who is 5'4" and wears a size 14 or 16, to models who average a size 2 and are 5'11"?

Moreover, it is getting worse…in 1985 the average model was a size 8, now the average model wears a size 0 or 2 (Betts, 2002). It is not only in body weight where women feel inferior, but also breast size, butt size, and the shape of their lips, eyes, chins, and cheekbones. Ask them and they can recite a list of their physical "defects" in detail: their pregnancy stretch lines, the cellulite on their thighs, their droopy breasts, their aging teeth, their flat butt, their facial wrinkles, dry skin and thinning hair.

The truth is that men find women of all sizes, colors, and shapes appealing and that it is often women who put most of the pressure on themselves.

What is really important to know though is that her perception of her body is her reality. In Areton's sexual satisfaction study, it was determined that the women's body image was not directly related to how much they weighed.

Darcy A. Cole

In other words, some heavier women felt better about their bodies than did the less heavy women.

It is a woman's perception of her body rather than the reality of her body that matters. What is good about this fact is that it can be much easier to change her perception of her body than to change her body.

Men can also be affected sexually by a poor body image. This is especially true if they don't think that they "measure up". Truthfully, the importance of penis size is vastly over-rated. One of my favorite scenes from the 2000 movie *What Women Want*, takes place when Mel Gibson tries to convey to his male coworker several startling facts he had learned ever since an accident gave him the ability to read the minds of females. After spending days listening to all of the private thoughts of women, Mel, expressing complete astonishment, tells his buddy that women don't have penis envy, only men do!

A woman can completely enjoy sex whether her partner's penis is small, large, thick or thin. The truth is that only 29% of women orgasm through intercourse anyway, according to Dr. Hutcherson (*Oprah* June 12, 2002). There are several tricks found in any number of sexual technique

Seduce Me!

books that take advantage of a man's specific size, whether big or small. Some positions, for instance would be very painful for a woman if her partner's penis were too large, but are very pleasurable with a smaller size. As the old saying goes, "It is not a matter of the size of the tool, it is knowing what to do with it that is important."

Implications. It is key for both men and women that body image not interfere in the anticipation or enjoyment of sex.

Our bodies do change over time, and usually not for the better. If your partner's body has changed in ways that cause him or her to not be as attractive to you, then that can also be a barrier that needs to be addressed.

The solution is to focus on the parts of his or her body that are attractive to you – her smile, her legs, etc. If she's gained a lot of weight, the only way she will lose it is if she cares enough about herself to do so. No one can do it for her and any negative comments from you will definitely not help. In the mean time, she needs to be convinced that she is still beautiful to you.

Darcy A. Cole

For men, there is no reason at all that a man can't become fully confident in his sexual capability, regardless of his penis size. If he's feeling inadequate, convince him otherwise. If there are difficulties, learn new techniques together.

Make your partner feel good about his or her body and you will not regret it! When we get to seduction scenes in Chapter 5, several can be helpful with building a more confident body image.

4. Sexual Inhibitions

In our society, girls are taught to be the sexual gatekeepers.

We're taught that boys will do or say anything to try to have sex and good girls don't let them. We're taught that boys don't respect girls that have sex. We're taught that giving in and having sex puts us at risk for emotional pain because he might just be "using" us for sex. We're taught to deny our natural sexual needs and desires and to marginalize girls who don't. That's pretty heady stuff for women to overcome.

The effects of these cultural messages can be more or less severe depending upon several other factors, including religious beliefs, parental values about and reactions to sex, and individual experiences with peers. Guilt, sexual inhibition, and sexual repression are some of the consequences of these experiences and they can interfere with our desire for and enjoyment of sex.

Other experiences that can inhibit our desire for sex include: conflict between our perceived roles as mothers and our sexual identities, confidence in our sexual abilities, and the degree to which past sexual experiences have been pleasurable and satisfying.

Men can also feel sexually inhibited. In addition to feelings about his penis size, some men try to avoid sex if they suffer from a lack of sexual confidence, performance anxiety, and the degree to which their past sexual experiences have been pleasurable and satisfying.

Men feel pressure to be the sexual aggressors and to know exactly what a woman needs. Unfortunately that is nearly impossible because every woman is different and what she enjoyed last night may not be what turns her on tonight.

Darcy A. Cole

Furthermore, female orgasms can be very complicated and they just aren't as easy to induce as are male orgasms. Yet a man may feel pressure to know how to make her orgasm, when in many cases she doesn't even know how herself.

Implications. Becoming free of these inhibitions is important for people to want and enjoy sex. This is especially true for women who don't have the powerful effects of testosterone to offset negative sexual feelings. For women, these issues can be like mental handcuffs that persist in blocking the joy of sexual freedom and pleasure. One key to resolving these issues is communication. Most couples, however, find it difficult to have discussions about sex. See Chapter 5 for some communication tips.

In many cases, men and women have never analyzed their beliefs and experiences to identify issues that are interfering with their sexual relationships. Some of us overcome these inhibitions on our own. Some of us take a little longer, and some of us require the help of a professional therapist to do so.

5. Frustrations/Resentments

Since women need to be seduced through their minds, lingering emotional frustrations and resentments can become major obstacles.

Negative emotions are like brick walls that stand in the way of her ability to become aroused. You can compare them to a blood vessel blockage in a man's penis. All of the stroking and visual stimulation you could imagine would be fruitless unless the blockage is removed and the blood could flow. In some ways, this is what happens with significant negative emotional issues.

Obviously, everyone has frustrations and resentments from time to time and they don't have to be completely alleviated in order to become aroused. On the other hand, it is difficult for her to clear her mind and become receptive to sex if she is pre-occupied with anger, resentment, frustration, hurt, worry, or sadness.

Moreover, emotional stress can decrease the desire for sex for both men and women because of its negative impact on prolactin, DHEA, and testosterone.

_____

Darcy A. Cole

Implications. If the issues are related to you or your relationship, then they need to be addressed. It's rare for couples to have good sex without a healthy relationship just as it's uncommon for couples to have a good relationship without sex.

Conflict is a necessary part of every relationship. Healthy relationships aren't those that don't have conflict, but those where the partners have developed good conflict resolution practices.

There are several resources to help couples with relationship management and conflict resolution including marital counseling, workshops, videos, and self-help books. Authors Harville Hendrix, David Burns, John Gray, Tony Robbins, and Phil McGraw offer great self-help tools. The Couples Center (http://www.couplescenter.com) also offers helpful guidelines for conflict resolution.

Universal conflict resolution tips include

- Don't expect your partner to have the gift of mind reading and be able to know why you're upset, or automatically know what you want from him. *"He should know that I need him to hug me when I'm sad."*

- Do not believe <u>you</u> have the gift of mind reading and assume you know why your partner did what he did. *"My health obviously isn't important to him because he knew I had this doctor's appointment today and didn't even ask me how it went."*

- Help your partner succeed at meeting your needs rather than setting up silent tests to demonstrate how much he cares about you and allowing him to fail. For instance, if he doesn't give you any indication that he is aware that your anniversary is coming up, then remind him, rather than waiting for him to fail and then making him feel guilty about it. You sabotage your relationship when you subject your partner to your tests for which he doesn't know the rules or that he's even taking a test. *"I'm not leaving him a note reminding him that my new aerobics class starts tonight; if he wonders why I'm not there when he gets home, it just proves he doesn't care about my schedule and he deserves to feel worried about where I am."*

- Develop good listening skills: look in your partner's eyes, listen fully without interrupting.

Darcy A. Cole

- Use feedback to ensure good communication: After your partner expresses his issue, repeat it back to him to make sure you understand what he is trying to communicate. *"So what you're saying is that when I buy something without telling you about it, you feel like I'm trying to spend money behind your back and undermine our savings goals."*

- Validate his feelings by expressing that you understand why he felt the way he did. *"You feel discounted when I don't call to tell you when I'm going to be late. I understand why you feel like that and I'm sorry."*

- Explain why you feel the way you do, then state the specific action you want from your partner, when and how often you need it to happen. Instead of saying, *"I need you to help around the house,"* state, *"I need you to vacuum the living room once a week."*

- Follow through with whatever you agree to do, and don't agree to do something that you aren't sure you can always do. Learn to negotiate a plan that you can both live with. *"I can't promise to call every time I'll be 10 minutes late, but I can promise to call when I'll be 20 or more minutes late. Will that work for you?"*

- Avoid yelling, blaming, name-calling, exaggerating, discounting feelings, using sarcasm, and arguing in front of the kids.

If your partner is upset about things that don't have anything to do with you, you can still help her by just listening to her recount the situation. Unless she asks for it, do not offer her advice or try to solve the problem for her. It is common for males and females to process negative emotions differently. Often females can resolve problems by having an attentive, validating partner listen to them, while men often need time alone to resolve theirs.

The bottom line is that over 50% of marriages end in divorce and the chances of having a successful relationship are dependent upon the couple's ability to negotiate and manage conflict.

6. Medical Obstacles

There are several medical issues that can interfere in a person's enjoyment of sex, including illnesses, medications (including anti-depressants), erectile dysfunction, pain with intercourse, lubrication problems, psychological issues and

---

Darcy A. Cole

depression, abuse issues, orgasmic disorders, and hormonal issues.

Implications. Medical issues are completely beyond the scope of this book. Comprehensive physical and psychosocial evaluations should be conducted by your doctor to rule out, or to identify and treat, any medical conditions. You can get referrals from your primary doctor, insurance company, or from several professional associations. Following are the website addresses for several associations that have referral services in addition to supplying very helpful information online.

- American Medical Association: <http://www.ama-assn.org>

- American Association for Marriage and Family Therapy: <http://www.aamft.org>

- American Association for Sex Educators Counselors and Therapists: <http://www.aasect.org>

- American College of Obstetricians and Gynecologists: <http://www.acog.org>

- American Psychiatric Association:
  <http://www.psych.org>

It is important to reiterate that we are talking in generalities about traditional roles that women and men have in our society. Some of these problems may apply to your situation and some may not. Some apply to both men and women. The object is to determine which of these obstacles interfere in your sexual relationship, understand how they hinder you, and take action to overcome them.

Seducing her mind is the key to igniting her passion and overcoming these mental obstacles is critical to getting her in tune with her sexual self. After overcoming the most potent mental obstacles—freeing her mind—then we can begin seducing her mind.

Ready to start seducing your partner?

---

4. The Seduce Me! Process

The secret to igniting your partner's passion is to evoke the intense desire you had for each other in the early days of your relationship. Remember how easy it was during those days when you couldn't wait to see each other and feel the touch of your partner's hands all over your body. In those moments, you were responding to the infatuation chemicals coursing through your body. These infatuation chemicals cause that "love high" feeling, triggering passionate sexual desire.

The pleasurable effects of these chemicals are so strong that some people jump from one relationship to another looking to experience the sensations over and over again. What these relationship jumpers don't realize is that it is possible to reproduce those sensations with their current partners, eliminating the need to go elsewhere to feel that love high.

Yes, it's true that as we move into the enduring love stage of our relationships the intense sensations of infatuation subside, but that doesn't mean that we can't reproduce those sensations during the enduring love stage! Better yet, we can do so for specific periods, any time we want.

We can stimulate an increase in the production of infatuation chemicals and inspire the passion that leads to sensational sex by creating scenarios that stimulate the brain's natural sexual impulses.

You've physically experienced their effects before, that suddenly warm-all-over feeling leading to stimulating sensations in your lower regions. Maybe you've felt them when you fantasized about someone, read a romance novel, watched a sex scene in a movie, heard an erotic poem, or saw a lustful look from an attractive stranger. These are the kinds of situations that can spark changes in our body's chemistry and stimulate our desire for sex.

Darcy A. Cole

The *Seduce Me!* process creates erotic mental experiences to increase sexual desire. What kinds of mental experiences? It depends on the person. What arouses one person can be different from what arouses another. The key is to determine which types of scenarios arouse you and your partner and then recreate them. We call them *tailored seduction scenes* because they are individually customized to stimulate your specific arousal systems — and they do so quite effectively!

Tailored seduction scenarios, which can consist of any number of activities, are the main ingredient of the *Seduce Me!* recipe for creating passion. Assuming mental obstacles have already been addressed, the *Seduce Me!* process involves the following steps

1. Date Night – A pre-scheduled block of time for just you and your partner

2. Seduction Scenario – Creating sexual and/or romantic events that arouse both partners

3. Bonding – Using the after-sex opportunity to increase emotional intimacy

4. Analysis – Continuously identifying ways to enhance each partner's pleasure

The *Seduce Me!* process is so exciting because it involves tailoring the evening to your needs. Unlike a one size fits all approach, this method is designed to fulfill whatever needs you and your partner have on a given evening. It will inspire intense passion, deliver hours of pleasure, and provide opportunities to deepen your level of intimacy. Furthermore, the process is self-enhancing with steps to make sure each time is better than the last.

In business graduate school, we're taught that the best managers are not those that can "tell time", but those that know how to "build a clock". In other words, rather than being the manager who is the only one who knows what course to take (a time teller), successful managers build internal systems so that *everyone* in the organization can determine the correct course to take (clock builders). The concept being it is better to have a system for self-learning than rely on the opinions of outside experts.

The *Seduce Me!* process uses the clock-building approach. *Seduce Me!* doesn't prescribe specific techniques for turning your partner on (the best way to perform oral sex, for instance), but instead delivers a process for

---

Darcy A. Cole

developing your own techniques that turn your partner on. Why? Because techniques that excite one man or woman may not excite another man or woman. Furthermore, what turns her on tonight may not turn her on tomorrow night. Great lovers figure out what excites their partners and then find ways of delivering. The *Seduce Me!* process shows you how to do just that.

Let's discuss each step in detail.

Step 1: Date Night

The importance of scheduling date nights for just the two of you cannot be emphasized enough. Our lives become so busy and we become so over-committed that it is virtually impossible for relationships to get the nourishment they need unless partners make it a point to do so.

Optimally you would have a date night at least once a week, but even a couple times per month is better than none. Depending upon the complexities of your schedules, date nights need to be planned far enough in advance that you are able to arrange your lives around them. It goes without saying that, once scheduled; you need to do all you can to avoid canceling or rescheduling date nights.

The guidelines for date night are: no friends, no family, no phone calls. To the extent possible, this needs to be uninterrupted time for the two of you. In addition to making your time together the priority it deserves, these guidelines help remove the guilt that the family nurturer often feels if she is not available to anyone who needs her when they think they need her.

Arrangements for childcare need to be such that you can both relax for the entire night, confidently assured that procedures are in place that would resolve most unforeseen situations without your involvement. Depending on the age of the children and babysitter, you need to designate a friend or relative as the substitute contact person for the evening. If you would normally check in with the babysitter at 9:00 pm, for instance, arrange to have your friend do so for you and to be available to your kids or sitter for the night.

Prepare the answering machine/voice mail for calls with a message that indicates when you will be able to return calls and whom to call in case of emergency.

_____

Darcy A. Cole

At first, friends and family who are used to you being available at a moment's notice will take some time getting used to you not being able to return calls until the next day, but they'll catch on soon enough. If you have any concerns about a specific person or situation, call them ahead of time and let them know you won't be available until the next day.

Of course, true emergencies do happen so it is best to give your substitute contact person the ability to get a hold of you. (Just make sure he or she knows what does and does not constitute an emergency!)

When selecting the location for your date night, choose somewhere away from home as often as possible, especially if you haven't had a date night in a while. Home can be very distracting with people coming to the door, phone calls, pets, kids, etc. Furthermore, you may have a hard time freeing her mind when many of the items on her mental checklist are staring her in the face. Alternate locations include a hotel room (it is easily worth the price), a friend's or relative's empty house, or the back row of a movie theater (JUST KIDDING! ....although the old drive-in theater has been known to serve a purpose!).

As you can see, date night helps to alleviate the common mental obstacle, emotional fatigue. Isolating her, without interruptions, frees her from her role as family nurturer, making her unavailable to those who normally turn to her whenever they choose. Activities that take place during date night will also help emotionally rejuvenate her.

Date night also addresses the common obstacle that we labeled "brain overload". Scheduling the night far enough in advance gives you both time to clear her checklist. As you come closer to the scheduled night, ask her what needs to be done so that she can feel free to take the night off, and then help her get the items resolved. Make another to-do list for what needs to be done the day after date night, so she doesn't spend her date night preoccupied with those responsibilities either. The purpose of date night is not to create more anxiety by giving her more to do, it is to give her the night off from her hectic life, so as much as you can do to help her get through the list, the better your night will be.

Date night should include dinner out (unless it would be considered seductive for the partner who rarely cooks to do so for his partner). Use dinner as a time to reconnect with each other emotionally. Remember why you fell in love with each other in the first place. Recall special moments in your relationship that stimulate loving feelings for each other. Some discussion topics for reconnecting are

- What you appreciate most about each other

- Some of the funniest moments you've shared

- The most romantic things you've done for each other

- What three things you find most attractive about each other

- The best presents you've ever given each other

- When you first realized you were in love

- What you admire most about your partner

- What were some of your best sexual moments together

- Three words that describe the best aspects of your partner's personality

- What dreams you have for your future together

Seduce Me!

- Three presents would you choose if you could give your partner anything in the world

- What your partner does that makes you feel loved

You can also use dinner to address any last minute issues that might have arisen. For instance, if either partner had a frustration at work earlier that day that is bothering him or her, take some time to address it, using listening techniques previously discussed. If the issue is going to interfere in either partner's ability to relax or escape for the night, then it needs to be addressed as best as possible.

This may seem like a lot of work, but remember that not giving your sexual relationship the priority it needs is how you got here in the first place. Trust me, it'll be worth it!

Step 2: Tailored Seduction Scenario

Tailored seduction scenarios include any activities specifically designed to arouse you and your partner. You create events that use sexual and/or romantic thoughts, visuals, emotions, fantasies, and touch that effectively ignite biochemical processes that arouse sexual desire. Some of us respond better to sexy visuals, others to romantic stories, and others to erotic touch.

Only you and your partner can determine what works best for you on a given night, understanding that your needs will change from time to time.

Following are six ways that you can use seduction scenarios to effectively ignite passion. This part of the date night can last anywhere from 30 minutes to 4 or 5 hours, depending on which seduction scene you use (and how much fun you're having!)

Acting out A Role-Play

Seduction role-plays are excellent ways to provoke sexual thoughts and feelings. You create erotic or romantic plots, with each partner pretending to be a specific character. There are an unlimited number of storylines that you can use (just think of how many romance novels or sexy movie themes there are) that very effectively arouse sexual desire. Common arousal themes are: new romantic love, a sexy encounter with a stranger, sex therapist, virgin and older man or woman, and voyeurism/exhibitionism.

In addition to arousing desire, role-playing is an effective tool because it helps slow down the pace of the typical bedroom sex of longer-term relationships. For instance, if you're acting out a role-play with a new romantic love theme, the aggressor knows he can't just start kissing and fondling his new partner. Instead, he's very patient, taking cues from her about how far he can go during the course of the evening. She plays "hard to get", controlling the pace as she would on a typical early date, while he keeps trying to get a little farther with each attempt.

Role-playing can also be very effective in addressing certain mental obstacles or inhibitions such as poor body image, shyness, inability to communicate likes and dislikes, and even differences in frequency of sex desired by two partners. In the next chapter, we provide several role-playing summaries and the seduction strategies they address.

Use the following guidelines to help make your role-playing scenes non-threatening and fully pleasurable for both partners.

Darcy A. Cole

- Select the theme and identify roles with one partner taking the lead and the other being somewhat resistant, in order to control the pace.

- Pick easy characters at first, those you're familiar with; you're not trying to win the actor of the year award, just get into the character and go with it.

- After determining scene and characters, give each other a little time to think through the roles and how they might be acted out.

- The degree to which you completely talk through the scene before you begin acting it out is dependent on you; some couples like the element of surprise and some prefer to know exactly where the seduction scene will end up.

- You can plan ahead and use several props (briefcase, clipboard, stethoscope, evening dress, tux, sleeping bag, etc.) or none at all.

- Pick a code word or hand signal that means "Stop the role-play now" and another that means "time-out," for when you need to temporarily get out of character for some reason. Use unusual words that wouldn't

———————————

Seduce Me!

come up in the role-play (such as "cabbage") or use your hands to make the T-sign as is done in football.

- Develop flow hints: be more aggressive, be less aggressive.

- Develop technique hints to instruct your partner (i.e., touch me here, harder, softer, faster, slower.) Use words or nonverbal cues. One method is to use exaggerated responses (i.e., moans and movement to indicate pleasure.) Don't make it complicated; if you're confused or want confirmation, just ask.

- Trust is vital especially in the beginning; avoid negative judgmental comments that demean your partner or his ideas (i.e., silly, perverted.)

- This is not time to get jealous, it is only make-believe. If any role-play theme seems risky to you, then choose another.

- Activities require joint agreement to proceed; this isn't the time to try to pressure your partner to participate in any activity for which he or she has clearly expressed aversion.

Darcy A. Cole

Have fun with these. Don't have expectations that the first few times will be perfect; they get easier over time.

Start with low-risk role-plays like the new romantic love theme and then experiment with bolder themes as desired. Look at the next chapter for some role-play ideas or invent some of your own by recalling erotic themes from your favorite movies or books or fantasies.

The only constraint is that the activities that take place during the role-play must have the full consent of both partners, and what takes place between two consenting adults is their own business. Couples who do these have a tremendous amount of fun experimenting with different themes, while inciting intense passion. So experiment and have fun.

Watching A Romantic or Sexual Movie

Women tend not to respond as well as men to traditional porn movies that focus purely on sex. Conversely, romantic movies don't always appeal to men. Now, however, producers are making sexual movies that have strong story lines to appeal to both men and women. Choose your movie type based on which partner needs help with arousal on this

particular night. Two websites,
<http://www.newshe.com/factsheets/erotic_videos_for_w
omen.shtml> and <http://www.bettersex.com> are among
those with access to erotic videos, including those tailored
more for women.

Erotic Massage

Remember that oxytocin levels increase with touch and
the higher our oxytocin levels, the more we want to be
touched. Massage is the answer, but not necessarily the kind
of massage you would get for sore muscles. Erotic massage
involves more caressing with light pressure.

To help your partner get aroused, plan to spend an hour
or two giving her a soft massage, making sure that you do
not touch either her breasts or her vaginal area until she is
ready or you may turn her off. Tell her that you will not
touch her anywhere she doesn't want you to until she gives
you signals that she's ready – and absolutely follow through
with that promise. Your primary goal is to help her fully
relax and allow the pleasurable sensations to permeate.
There are many good instructional videos available,
including *Intimate Loving: Massage For Lovers (2000)*.

Darcy A. Cole

Playing Games

There are several fun games that help with sexual arousal. Games range from romantic and light hearted like "An Enchanted Evening" to risqué and kinky like "Intimate Commands". For hours of fun, try "Fore-Playing Cards," especially if you like poker.

You can find these and other adult games at Bippy (http://www.bippy.com/gamesncards.htm) and Bridal Shower Fun (www.bridalshowerfun.com/adultgames.htm). With a bit of creativity, you can invent your own games out of dozens of everyday activities. Here are three creative games that you can tailor

- *Points for football scores:* Each partner picks a team and then together they put together a point system (points for sacks, interceptions, touchdowns, field goals). Points are then converted to favors as agreed to by both partners before the game begins (massage for 5 minutes, long hug, passionate kiss, slow strip, neck nibbles, etc.) If one team is expected to totally dominate the other, even the playing field by giving the partner with the weaker team extra points before the game starts.

- *Points for Oscar Picks:* Same idea as for football games, but these points are earned for correctly picking Oscar winners. Ahead of time, both partners need to have seen the top nominated movies. Points are awarded for correctly picking the winners of Best Picture, Best Actress, Best Actor, Best Director, Best Supporting Actor, Best Supporting Actress, and for any other categories you decide. As in the football points game, convert the points to favors.

- *Must pay attention to movie:* This is a fun game to play, especially if a good movie is on TV. Each partner takes 10-minute turns sensually teasing the other's body. The rule is that the partner must not close his or her eyes and has to focus on the movie while being teased. After 10 minutes, the partners switch and the second partner watches the movie while the first partner teases the other's body. This goes on for an hour or more until both partners feel abundantly aroused and are ready to move on.

Re-enacting a Previous Exciting Event

This is a form of role-playing except you are playing yourselves by re-enacting an exciting time or date that took place during the infatuation stage of your relationship. You don't have to remember everything word for word, but remember the sense of excitement and anticipation you felt for each other. This type of seduction scenario is also a great introduction to role-playing.

Reading Or Telling a Romantic or Erotic Story

The romance novel market is so tremendously large for a good reason. Reading aloud or making up and telling romantic and/or erotic stories are very effective in helping women conjure up sexual images. Because of testosterone, men are typically better at fantasizing on their own, whereas women sometimes need a little help.

It's difficult to read a full-length novel during the course of one evening, but there are several smaller paperbacks, short stories, and books on cassette that could substitute.

You can find many erotic books at adult bookstores. Several websites specialize in erotic reading materials,

Seduce Me!

including <http://www.eroticaforwomen.com> and <http://www.booksforwomen.netfirms.com>.

Some are more explicit than others, so you have to choose one that suits your tastes. The object is to become immersed in the story, visualizing the characters and the scenes in order to spark the chemicals that increase arousal. Some people are great story creators or storytellers and can make them up on their own. This is also a good way to set the stage for role-playing.

Experiment with these seduction tools to learn which are most effective for you and your partner. If you have identified specific arousal challenges, review the next chapter for ways that seduction scenes can help. In addition, a fully scripted role-play is included at the end of the next chapter.

Step 3: Bonding

After sex, hormones and neurotransmitters (i.e., oxytocin, endorphin) have been activated that can help us strengthen our emotional bonds. This is a good time to hug, touch, talk, and be loving with each other. Avoid feeling compelled to get up and do anything; just lay there and feel good together. Allow yourselves time to let the euphoric feelings permeate, associating those positive associations with your partner.

Because of the heightened sensations, beware of the types of emotional associations you're creating with your partner. Emotional associations are things (people, places, sounds, smells, items) that can evoke emotional memories because they were present when a strong emotion was experienced. They can be positive emotional associations or negative, and we often have no idea that we've created them.

For example, one individual spent over two decades puzzled by her irrational fear of bees and wasps until she one day remembered an event that had clearly caused her to subconsciously associate terror with their presence. Only 10 years old and hiding in an old shed from her mother's enraged boyfriend, she suddenly looked up to find several wasps buzzing around a nest just above her head. Terrified of giving away her location she remained frozen for several minutes until she heard the volatile boyfriend finally give up and leave the shed. This event caused her to associate bees and wasps with the feeling of tremendous fear. Although she had forgotten the root source, the association was powerful enough for her to maintain a subconscious terror of bees and wasps for over 25 years!

Emotional associations can be created over several occasions or, as the wasp story demonstrates, be powerful enough to be created with just one event. You've experienced emotional associations when a song on the radio lifts your mood or the tone of your voice changes when you answer the phone to find a telemarketer interrupting your dinner. Corporations spend billions of dollars relying on the subconscious emotional associations of consumers when they hire celebrities to appear in ads holding or using their products.

The stronger your emotional state, the stronger the emotional association, which is why the time following sex is important. Use this time to make sure you're creating, or re-enforcing, positive emotional associations with each other. Doing or saying anything negative could spoil your partner's experience and create new barriers you'd have to address in order to have great sex next time.

Darcy A. Cole

Step 4: Analysis

At some point, you want to review and analyze date
night and the seduction scene so you can continue to learn
about each other and improve the process. Many couples
find it very difficult to talk about sex. Here are some
questions to get the discussion started.

- What did you like most about the scene?

- Which parts were most exciting to you?

- If we do a similar themed scene, what is another path
we can take that would be exciting?

- What signals did I read right or did I miss?

- What did you mean when you did this?

- What different/better signals can I use?

- What are some other scenes that would be exciting
(think of movies, books, past events that are sexually
exciting to you)?

The least threatening way to communicate is by
emphasizing what you enjoyed most and de-emphasizing

what you didn't. Don't bombard him or her with your list for improvements – tackle no more than one or two at a time – this is a gradual process and you need to build each other's confidence. Use the oft-recommended 10 to 1 rule: 10 positives for every one negative. Here are some other tips for communicating with each other

1. Start with equal understanding that everybody is different and it is unrealistic to expect each other to automatically KNOW each other's likes and dislikes.

2. Ask your partner how he or she wants you to communicate your preferences. What form of communication would he prefer (verbal, hand-guiding, body language), and when would be the best time to communicate preferences (before, during, after sex).

3. Be cognizant of each other's egos. Don't attack, exaggerate, compare to previous lovers, insult, or in any other way demean your partner.

4. People enjoy doing what they feel that they are good at doing. Find ways to increase his or her confidence

_____

Darcy A. Cole

by pointing out what your partner does that you really enjoy.

Remember that Areton's sexual satisfaction study demonstrated that the best predictor of sexual satisfaction is sexual communication. The Sinclair Institute (http://www.bettersex.com) informs us however, that only 41% of women report having discussed sex with their partners. Learning how to communicate each other's needs, likes, and dislikes in a non-threatening manner is the best step you can take to have sensational sex.

It's not too late!

Sometimes, especially if there has been a long period of unresolved sexual difficulties, one partner has developed significant negative associations with sex. She hasn't been interested in sex for a long time and feels pressure to get aroused, or guilty for not getting aroused. She looks for ways to avoid sex altogether. Many report that they've become reluctant to even hug their partners fearing it be mistaken as a signal for sex. In these cases, just learning that there may be biological reasons for low libido can help remove the guilt she's felt for so long.

When you're both ready to try the *Seduce Me!* process, it's important to remove any pressure she feels to become aroused and have sex. In order to counteract the power of this significant mental block, several date nights without having any expectations of having sex may be required. Have several opportunities to reconnect emotionally, using the sample questions listed previously.

Erotic massage can be especially effective if she has long felt pressured to have sex or to get aroused and hasn't been able to. Tell her that there are no expectations for sex. This helps her let down her guard, let go of feeling pressured or feeling like she will disappoint you if she doesn't get aroused. Remember also that touch releases oxytocin, which makes us want to be touched even more. Even so, it may take a few separate occasions of erotic massage before she's ready. In the mean time, make date night enjoyable for both of you.

_____

Darcy A. Cole

5. Seduction Scene Strategies

As you gain experience, you can use role-playing to address specific sexual situations that can be obstacles to fully experiencing the pleasures of intimacy and passion. Again, addressing medical issues is beyond the scope of this book. Many couples, however, have found role-plays to be a great way to ease barriers that inhibit full sexual enjoyment.

Following are common obstacles and seduction strategies, with sample role-play themes to counteract them. For convenience, roles are described using "he" and "she", but in no manner does that mean that the roles can't be switched. Review, experiment and alter them to fit your own tastes, but above all, have fun!

Seduce Me!

It is important to understand that role-plays are make-believe and are in no way a measure of a person's true desires. For instance, initiating a sex slave fantasy does not mean she wants to be treated as a sex slave in a non-fantasy setting. Submission fantasies are really about an individual participating in certain sexual acts without "owning" her actions, thereby freeing her from any internal judgments about what she is doing. Likewise, rape fantasies, which occur in 36% of women (and about 24% of men), are really about her feeling desirable, in addition to avoiding responsibility for sexual acts (Crenshaw, 1996; Knox, 1984; Tucker-Ladd, 1996).

The strategies that the following role-plays address are

- Slowing the pace

- Improving body image

- Gradual romantic seduction

- Acting out exhibitionist/voyeur fantasies

- Providing extra pampering

- Overcoming negative sexual messages

Darcy A. Cole

- Using role reversal

- Handling differences in desire for sex

- Learning each others likes and dislikes

- Learning about G-spot and female ejaculation

Slowing the Pace

There are two types of "slowing the pace" role-plays. One is character-based where one character is resistant to the other's advances. These let the resistor control the pace while the seducer keeps trying to accelerate the progress. The other type is theme-based, where steps are implemented to control the pace of both characters.

Longest Foreplay Competition

Two competitive co-workers are working on a marketing campaign plan for massage oil. During the course of their meetings, they become flirty, teasing each other about which of them is more attracted to the other. He says things like "Well, we better finish up because I can tell you

_____

want me and I don't want to drive you so crazy that you can't sleep tonight." She responds with, "Just because you stay up all night dreaming about me doesn't mean the feeling is mutual."

The teasing leads to the topic of foreplay and which of them has the best foreplay techniques. He brags that he could excite her to the point that she would be begging him for intercourse. She counters with claims that her excellent skills would have him ready to screw anything that moved before a moan even escaped her lips.

This goes on during the course of their work project for some time before he finally challenges her to prove her claim. After figuring out how to make it worth her while, she decides to accept the challenge, suggesting that the loser would have to stay awake for the rest of the night to finish preparing the marketing plan for the next day's presentation. He agrees to the bet but advises her to make a pot of coffee for herself, so she doesn't fall asleep working all night on the presentation.

They decide that he will start by taking a 15-minute turn at using his foreplay techniques on her. Then, she will use her best foreplay on him for the next 15 minutes. They

Darcy A. Cole

decide that this will go on back and forth until one of them either orgasms or concedes by asking the other to make them orgasm. (Eventually he teases her to the point where she begs and he wins – but knowing how close he was to losing, he offers to work together to finish the report!)

College Students in Film Class

Two college students have been assigned a final project for their film class. They have to watch a specific movie together and then answer the questions on a form. The two students have liked each other for a while but have never dated. During the course of the movie, they start flirting with each other leading to a kiss. They want to continue kissing and exploring each other, but it is critical that they pay attention and watch the whole movie in order to complete the assignment.

Lesbian French Maid

She is a lesbian maid with a French accent. He is a lonely single who meets her at a hotel lobby. She just broke up with her girlfriend and is sad, but has never been with a man before. He is very attracted to her and wants to convince her

Seduce Me!

that he can do everything her girlfriend did and better. She is reluctant because she doesn't want him to feel bad when he can't be as good as her old girlfriend. He keeps pressing on and eventually convinces her to let him try…and she becomes glad he did.

Improving Body Image

These role-plays help her feel good about her body as her partner works hard to convince her that she is beautiful and desirable just the way she is. These can be altered for any body part…breasts that are small, large, or saggy, hips, facial wrinkles, cellulite, disfigurement, stomach, etc.

Pre-Surgery Interview

She has small breasts and wants to have implants because she feels that she looks horrible. He is the plastic surgeon conducting the pre-surgery interview. He examines her and tells her that not only are her breasts not horrible, but that they're beautiful and that he refuses to operate on her. She remains unconvinced for a very long time until he finds ways to show her how her beautiful body affects him.

Darcy A. Cole

Victoria's Bigger Secrets

He's a photographer for a new lingerie magazine called "Victoria's Bigger Secrets" for plus size women. She's having difficulty getting ready to be the model and he truly convinces her that she looks beautiful and sexy as she tries on different pieces of lingerie for the photos.

Therapist Helps with Body Issues

She believes her naked body is hideous and refuses to let any man see it – which has created a few problems in her relationships. He is a psychiatrist who, over the course of several hours, helps to convince her that her naked body is beautiful and desirable to men, especially him.

Gradual Romantic Seduction

These role-plays can spark an increase in those infatuation chemicals that make us feel sexual. They're also great for slowing the pace.

Neighbor with Electricity Failure

It's the night of the big game and suddenly he has electrical failure. He knocks on her door and asks if she'll let him watch the game with her at her apartment. They've known each other for a while, but other than harmless flirtation in the hallway of their apartment building, they haven't yet dated. He is very seductive and slowly makes his move on her. She thinks he's gorgeous and is very excited by his seductive ways, but resists him because she doesn't want him to get the impression that she is easy.

Strangers Caught in Winter Storm

Two strangers meet while hiking a mountain when suddenly they're caught in a freak snowstorm. They find an abandoned cabin, but with soaking wet clothes and only one dry blanket to share, they have to rely on shared body heat to keep them alive. Although they're both kind of shy, eventually they find several ways to make heat and stay warm.

Darcy A. Cole

Third Date Seduction

He wants her. She wants him, but she believes good girls wait before having sex, and they've only had two dates. While sitting on her couch watching a movie, he lets his hand wander very subtly trying to see how far he can get. She lets him go only so far, before she silently moves his hand back on her shoulder. Each time he tries though, she lets him go a little further than the time before. All of this takes place while they pay close attention to movie. Eventually his seduction becomes too much for her to resist on this night.

UPS Delivery Man

She's a writer living alone in the mountains for the summer to finish her book. He's the UPS deliveryman. He makes deliveries once or twice a week. Every time he shows up, she is wearing something sexier and more revealing than the time before. She seems oblivious to how sexy she looks or the effect it has on him when she does things like brushing against him while signing his clipboard, or asking his help in putting some sunscreen on her back. They start flirting and eventually during one delivery, she invites him to come over for dinner the next night. When he arrives

_____

Seduce Me!

early and rings her doorbell, she comes running from the shower wearing only a towel....

Double Booked at Fantasy Suite

They meet because the hotel made a serious mistake and booked them for the same romantic room/cottage for the same weekend. They both have a key to the room and find that there are no other suites available. Since they're both feeling a bit depressed because they've each broken up with the person they were originally supposed to share the fantasy suite with, they eventually decide to make the best of it and enjoy the room together.

Seductive Personal Trainer

He's the sexy personal trainer who makes house calls. She's the quiet student with the biggest crush on him. With every movement of his body, she becomes more enamored. When he touches her to show her the right exercise, techniques she practically melts. He has no idea of the effect he has on her, but catches her getting distracted and staring at him several times. Finally, when the session is nearly over she hints about her secret crush for him and he, never

---

Darcy A. Cole

wanting a client to feel less than fully satisfied with his services, takes care of her secret fantasies.

Acting out Exhibitionist/Voyeur Fantasies

Voyeur roles are effective because sexy visuals can increase testosterone thereby increasing sex-drive, while acting as a confident exhibitionist can help improve body image. It's the old "fake it till you make it" trick.

Packing Suitcase Exhibitionist

They're coworkers who have to go to a weeklong planning meeting at a resort. She's never been to the annual meeting and so he comes over to her house to help her pick out various outfits she'll need while they're there (i.e., evening dress, golf outfit, bathing suit, casual clothes).

Even though there is nothing romantic between them, she is a bit of an exhibitionist and likes the reaction she gets as she changes clothes in front of him. He is shocked that she keeps changing clothes right in front of him. At first he politely looks away, but eventually realizes that if she doesn't mind him watching her then why should he?

_____

Seduce Me!

Handyman

He is the handyman that she found in the phone book to help her put up her new drapes. She is lonely and a bit of an exhibitionist and tries to distract him from his job. He is somewhat reserved, but can't help but peek when she parades around half dressed and brushes against him as he is working. Enjoying the evening, it ends up taking him much longer than it normally does to install drapes. Eventually, she becomes too much to resist and decides to see how far she's willing to go.

Dancer Tryout

She is desperate for money so she tries out to be a dancer at a strip club in the city. She never been a dancer, but she's willing to try. He's the manager of the club and he's conducting the auditions for new dancers. She clearly doesn't have much experience, but he wants to hire her so he gives her instruction about what clothes make her look sexiest and how to dance in the sexiest ways, while boosting her confidence with a lot of positive feedback.

Darcy A. Cole

Providing Extra Pampering

This is a great role-play for times when she is exceptionally stressed or anytime he wants to treat her especially well. Of course, the roles can always be reversed!

Spa Owner

He owns the spa and personally gives her the best and most relaxing day of her life. She is entirely exhausted after a hard day's work and visits a private spa designed to fully pamper women. Spa treatment includes: personally giving her a warm shower and shampoo (she keeps eyes closed to relax them); softly drying her from head to toe; a full body massage, with a warm towel over eyes for relaxation; foot and hand massage leading to a full frontal massage.

PMS & Unique Treatment

She gets horrendous PMS every month that leaves her with extremely painful breasts. No other treatment has worked, so she goes to this unorthodox doctor who promises a 100% cure rate. His treatments involve a lot of massaging, however. She decides she's desperate enough to

Seduce Me!

give it a try. It turns out that the massaging not only relieves the PMS discomfort, but brings a lot of pleasure as well.

Overcoming Negative Sexual Messages

These role-plays help counteract negative messages that interfere in a woman's enjoyment of sex, such as "sex is dirty" or "aggressive women are sluts" messages. One reason women like acting out role-plays where she is under his control (or vice versa) is because she doesn't have to own any sexual acts (i.e., she was just doing what she was told to do). Another form of "naughty" sex that is fun to act out in role-plays are those that involve having sex with someone you know but aren't involved with romantically.

Psychiatrist Helps Overcome Inhibitions

He's a psychiatrist who is known for one-session cures. She goes to see him because she hates sex and can't keep a relationship going for longer than a few months. During the course of their therapy session, he discovers that she thinks sex is "dirty" because when she was a teenager she was caught kissing a boy by her mother, who drummed it into

---

Darcy A. Cole

her head that sex was disgusting and she would go to hell if she thought about sex ever again. He needs to convince her that her mother was wrong and that sex is a healthy and necessary part of a good relationship. In the process, he shows her that she is a sexual woman and that with a good partner, sex can be very pleasurable.

Lawyers & Quid Pro Quo

They are lawyers who are opponents on a case about fraud, where her elderly clients were cheated out of their savings. She is trying to get tidbits of information from him in order to help her clients.

He agrees to give her a piece of information but she has to reciprocate – quid pro quo – by giving him something he wants – starting with a kiss, then a hug and then moves on from there – each trade is negotiated. She finds the idea of using sex to get information repulsive, but she's desperate to help her clients. Besides, it might not be too bad; she's hasn't had a date in years and always had a little bit of a crush on him anyway.

Undercover Prostitute Training

He is a detective in the sex crimes division of the police department. She's recently graduated from the police academy. She has the looks he needs to go undercover as a prostitute, but being from a small town, she has no idea of how to imitate a prostitute. He teaches her how to dress and behave as a prostitute, for which, it turns out, she has a previously undiscovered talent.

Competitive Coworkers & Winning Games

Two co-workers are very competitive. They make bets constantly on everything imaginable. They're away on a business trip and get into a conversation about who is the most skilled at winning games – card games, regular board games, dice games, physical games.

She challenges him to a bet that he can pick any game he chooses and she will beat him at it. He takes the bet because he plans to trick her; the game he has in mind is a sex related board game. When they get back to his room, he springs the surprise. She is at first taken aback, but has too much pride to let him win…and so the game begins.

Darcy A. Cole

Naughty Hypnotist

She sees a hypnotist in order to quit smoking. He finds that under hypnosis, she's very cooperative in doing anything he tells her to do.

Role-Reversal

Women are acculturated to be sexually demure and inhibited. With these role-reversal themes, she's the aggressive one. These can effectively get her in the mood for sex as long as he is *very* resistant to her moves. In acting as the aggressor, she has to be sure that he won't quickly give-in before she's had the chance to want him long enough.

Lonely Widow & Shy Lawn Mowing Young Man

She's the attractive but lonely widow who wants to feel young again. He's the young man she hired to mow her lawn. She's a bit aggressive, and he's a bit shy. But it doesn't take too much convincing him to let her lead him to her bedroom.

Seduce Me!

Wicked IRS Agent

He runs his own business, but seems to have made several big mistakes on his tax returns. She's the IRS agent who finds her own self-fulfilling ways for him to avoid severe penalties and/or jail.

Aggressive Woman and Shy Guy in Pool

He's immensely shy. She's immensely horny. They first meet at the hotel pool where she does everything in her power to get this shy but cute man up to her room. He can't believe his luck, but he's afraid to go up to her room and get embarrassed because he has very little sexual experience. He wonders if she is just teasing him, or is it possible she really does want to have sex with him? It takes a lot of convincing before he finally takes the plunge and follows her up to her room.

Handling Differences in Desire for Sex

As detailed in Chapter 2, sex can enhance the relationship, as well as providing several individual health benefits. Every couple faces periods where one partner

---

wants sex more often than the other, or when one wants sex and the other can't physically have sex. It's nice to have some role-plays that help in these situations.

Maintenance Man Voyeur

He's the apartment complex maintenance man who is changing all of the door handles in her apartment. Because he knows she won't be home for another hour or so, he takes the opportunity to peek in her drawers. Suddenly he hears her come in the front door and afraid of getting caught in her bedroom, he hides in the closet, leaving the door cracked open so he doesn't make any noise closing it. From there, he watches and masturbates as she undresses and continues with her normal activities, unknowingly putting on quite a show for him.

Massage Therapist with Extra Skills

She's very shy and never had a full body massage before, but he comes highly recommended and so she decides to try it out – although she's not fully sure what to expect. He's a very skilled masseur who can tell that she is gullible. During the long massage, he manages to subtly

Seduce Me!

excite her body to the point where she can't stand it any more and then he brings her to orgasm.

Caught By Mother's Friend

He is an inexperienced college student living at home with his mother and she is his mother's friend (older woman, but still sexy). She's temporarily staying at his mom's house and accidentally walks in on him masturbating.

He begs her not to tell his extremely prudish mother who would be horrified. She agrees not to tell his mother, but seeing how repressed his mother is making him, she decides that he deserves to see how a woman can pleasure him without even getting undressed.

Learning Each Other's Likes and Dislikes

Many couples find that using a seduction scene can communicate sexual desires by alleviating the common communication deterrents: shyness or embarrassment, a fear of hurting their partner's feelings, and the inability to identify their own body's needs and desires. Several themes

---

Darcy A. Cole

can help identify desires and communicate them in a non-threatening manner.

For example, acting out a sexual therapist role-play would require one partner to "instruct" the other partner about methods to please the opposite sex. When acting out these roles, a shy person can take the role as the more experienced character and give the other partner specific direction about what they like and dislike.

Sex Therapist

He feels inadequate in bed and is afraid to date anyone. She's a professional sex therapist who shows him many different ways to please a woman by paying attention to and interpreting the hidden clues that a woman's body gives during sex.

Blind Woman

He works for an organization that helps blind people with day-to-day living activities (reading mail, grocery shopping, etc.). She's an inquisitive woman whose former female helper moved out of the area. Having never explored the male form, once she meets her new helper and realizes

Seduce Me!

he is a male, she is determined to satisfy her curiosity. He is resistant because of his professional code of ethics; however, she is very beautiful and maybe he'll let her explore for just a minute or two and then he'll make her stop…or will he?

Virgin

She's an adult virgin who knows nothing about a man's body but is anxious to learn. He guides her step by step through everything she could do to please a man, and take care of her own needs as well.

New Adult Store Manager

He is a single man who has just become manager of an adult bookstore and feels inadequately informed about all of the products. She is a good college friend who offers to teach him what little she knows, and explore with him the products she's not tried before. Together they learn all kinds of new tricks and find out their friendship grows to a new level.

Darcy A. Cole

Learning about G-Spot &Female Ejaculation

G-Spot Experiment

He is a busy, but somewhat shy medical researcher trying to learn about the g-spot and female ejaculation. She is his girlfriend, although he's been so busy that they haven't yet had sex with each other (much to her dismay). She doesn't know anything about the g-spot either, but she's willing to help him with his research, especially if it means she can finally have his undivided attention focused on her body.

Together they watch a video that explains the g-spot and different techniques to find and stimulate it, and then they practice the techniques. Since they are both new to the g-spot concept, neither feels any pressure to "perform". If it works, great; if not, at least she finally "got in his pants."

Briefly, the g-spot is the common name for an area in the vagina where you can feel underlying glands, often referred to as the "female prostrate". Upon arousal, the female prostrate swells and can be felt more easily through the

Seduce Me!

inside front wall of the vagina. With direct pressure, the g-spot is a source of immense pleasure, often culminating in intense orgasm accompanied by expulsion of fluid. This clear and odorless fluid, female ejaculate, has been proven to be neither urine nor vaginal lubrication (although small amounts of both can get mixed into it).

Honoring Dr. Grafenberg, who published detailed initial research in 1950, the area was named the "Grafenberg Spot" by authors Perry, Whipple, and Ladas in their landmark 1982 book, *The G-Spot and Other Recent Discoveries about Human Sexuality.*

The g-spot and female ejaculation is still controversial, although historians have found reference to the area and the ability of women to secrete these fluids in writings as far back as Hippocrates. In 1997, Dr. Santamaria presented his research, *Female Ejaculation, Myth and Reality*, determining that as many as 75% of women expel some quantity of female ejaculate during orgasm, in amounts anywhere from barely noticeable drops to fully gushing streams.

A woman may find her g-spot if she squats (on the toilet, for instance) and, partially inserting two fingers, curls them as if to tickle the inside front wall of her vagina. It is about

---

Darcy A. Cole

one or two inches in and feels ridged and spongy. Her partner would have more success finding the g-spot if she lays on her back with her knees up and he sits next to her facing the same direction so that when he inserts his two fingers his hand is facing up just behind the clitoris. The back of his fingers and knuckles would be against the back wall of her vagina angled toward her anus, where she might also feel some pressure.

Stimulate the g-spot with rhythmic pressure of the fingers, either through direct poking or stroking, or rubbing in a circular motion. As she gets aroused, the area swells, sometimes to the size of a small, soft walnut. At some point, she may feel the urge to urinate, which is completely normal. She should not try to hold back or resist the sensation. In fact, it is believed that a major reason that some women do not regularly ejaculate is that, fearing that they are about to urinate, they mentally shut down, blocking further progress.

If she feels like she has to urinate, increase the rate of g-spot stroking, while she allows the feeling to build, or even pushes down as if she were trying to urinate. Do not worry; it's virtually impossible for men to urinate during orgasm, and likely the same for women (Hicks, 2001). During g-spot orgasm, he may feel her vagina tighten around his fingers (or penis) almost to the point of being pushed out. The amount of ejaculate varies, but can be quite a lot, so couples use a towel over a rubber bath mat to contain it. Don't be too bothered if some fluid gets on the bed, however, because, unlike urine, it dries leaving no odor or stain.

There is an abundance of resources for couples that want to explore the g-spot and female ejaculation, including

Books:

- The G-Spot And Other Recent Discoveries About Human Sexuality by Ladas, Whipple, & Perry;

- Understanding the G-Spot and Female Sexuality: A Simple 10-Step Guide for Unleashing the Ultimate in Female Ecstasy by Donald L. Hicks

- The G-Spot - The Good Vibrations Guide by Cathy Winks

Videos:

- A Guide to the G Spot & Extreme Multiple Orgasms

- The Amazing G-Spot and Female Ejaculation

Websites:

- <http://www.very-koi.net/tutor/female/female.htm

- <http://www.DoctorG.com>

- <http://www.drgspot.net>

- <http://www.libchrist.com/sexed/Gspot.html>

When it comes to female orgasm, remember that only 29% of women experience orgasm through intercourse, so the chances of having one without additional clitoral and/or g-spot stimulation aren't high.

Many women say that they are unsure if they've ever had an orgasm or are positive they've never had one. Should couples experiment in an effort to help her achieve orgasm? Absolutely. Most experts recommend she attempt to do so first through masturbation. A very informative site about female orgasm is <http://www.clitical.com>

The last thing a couple needs to do is to put pressure on her to have an orgasm. As with males, performance anxiety interferes with our ability to relax and enjoy sex. When experimenting with g-spot or clitoral orgasms, do so only as

Seduce Me!

long as it is enjoyable for both. If she feels like she has disappointed either or both of you by not having an orgasm, your efforts to have sensational sex may backfire.

While g-spot orgasms provide great pleasure, even women who regularly experience them still greatly enjoy sex on occasions that they don't orgasm.

It is tempting for women to fake orgasms to remove pressure and to make her partner feel better. Just don't. In the end, faking orgasms only hurts the relationship and if he erroneously believes he has the right technique to make her orgasm, they both lose out because he doesn't feel the need to try different approaches.

Fully Scripted Seduction Scene

The seduction role-plays that have been described in this chapter are meant to give you ideas to start the process. You can tailor them to your tastes, making them last for anywhere from 30 minutes to several hours. Following is an example of a fully scripted role-play, where he is resistant to her suggestive behavior.

Seductive Secretary Wanting a Job from the Cautious Executive

She's a secretary sent over by the temp agency and he's the executive in urgent need of a secretary because he's working on a big project. It's Saturday and she's been sent to his office to help him meet the project's important deadline.

She desperately wants to be hired as his permanent secretary and she has two strategies: 1) to demonstrate that she is a competent secretary with all of the skills required to do the job and 2) to use her feminine charm to convince him that the office would be far more interesting if she was there on a full time basis. A conservative professional businessman, he's never before been in he position of being "hit on" by a sexy secretary. He's not sure how to react except that he's had enough corporate training to know that responding inappropriately could cost him his job and career.

The executive is sitting in his desk in front of a computer, looking at papers. Smiling and optimistic, she walks in the office wearing a short skirt and seductive low cut blouse. "Hi, the temp agency sent me over. They said you had a big deadline today."

Seduce Me!

"Yes I do, I hope you can help me with this project; I haven't yet replaced my secretary who retired last week and I'm desperate to get this job done. I'm so glad that the temp agency had someone they could send in on a Saturday."

"Great, well I'm willing to help in any way I can. What can I do first?"

His first request was to see if she could find some research literature in the bookcase – he thinks it's on the bottom shelf. She bends over from the waist with her back to him exposing the back of her upper thighs. Although he's pleasantly surprised with the view, he's afraid to get caught peeking, so he quickly looks away.

She finds the book he was looking for and then places it on the desk in front of him – and in the process, she lightly brushes her chest against his shoulder. "Is this the one you were looking for?" she asks innocently.

"Um, err yes," he says. Neither of them makes any indication that they noticed the brief contact and continue as if nothing happened.

The boss, having enjoyed the experience, suddenly remembers another research item he needs and sends her back to the bookcase to look for it. This time, she bends even lower from the waist and provides him with a more revealing view, including a hint of her panties. "Hmmm I'm having a hard time finding this book; you said the title has something to do with marketing strategies? Is it a hardcover book?"

"Uh yes…I mean no…. it's…. um… a report in a binder." Her search takes longer this time and he stops what he is doing so he can take full advantage of the view. "Yeah that's the one," he says, somewhat disappointed, when she finds it and just hands it to him.

"Glad to help, what else can I do for you?" she smiles sweetly. Looking over his shoulder at the papers on his desk, she asks, "Is this the report you need me type?"

"Yes, but before I can give it to you, I need to know what these notes are in the margin and I'm having a hard time reading the writing."

"Oh I'm good at that…let me see," she says as she bends over, leaning into his arm to get a closer look at the papers. Stunned, he tries not to move, pretending that he doesn't notice her chest against his arm. As she looks even closer at

Seduce Me!

the paper, her upper body presses harder against his arm and shoulder.

"Hmmm this writing IS really hard to read." She presses closer. "This note here," pointing at the paper, "says to 'add more detail to the consumer profile' and this one says to 'delete the last section on page 4'. Does that make sense to you? "

"Oh, uh... yeah ... that's right," he says, somewhat flustered. "I think there's a few more notes on these other pages you could help me with also."

This goes on for a few minutes with her bending over to read and decipher the notes, sometimes pressing against him, sometimes not. Finally, she asks, "Do you have someone in mind to replace your retired secretary?"

"No, and I've been so busy with this project that I haven't had a chance to interview anyone yet!"

"Really, because I'd like to apply for the position. I have many skills and I'd really appreciate the chance to show you how good I am. Haven't I been helpful so far?" she asks.

Darcy A. Cole

"Yes you've been just perfect. I'd love to hire you now, but I'm required to go through the regular procedures and interview several other candidates. But so far, you seem to be very good at what you do."

She replies that she's more than just very good and if he'll give her the chance, she can show him that she's an outstanding secretary. She makes it clear that she'd be *extremely* appreciative if he hired her. "Now, are you ready for me to start typing that report yet?"

"Yes, but I have to get someone from the computer department to come up here because I've been having problems with the printer. I hope the computer techs work on Saturdays!"

As he starts to reach for the phone, she stops him, "Wait, that may not be necessary. Let me take a look at it first." She steps in between him and the desk. "Let me just get a look at the back of the computer to see if the printer is connected right." She bends down over his legs to reach for the computer that is under his desk.

He inhales sharply. "Uh…OK, be my guest." For the next several minutes, she moves up and down and around

---

Seduce Me!

his legs as she checks the computer and printer wires and plugs, removing and replacing them in the various sockets. During the process, various parts of her body come in direct contact with various parts of his as she intently concentrates on trying to fix the printer and impress him with all of her "attributes."

At first, the boss is stunned at her boldness, but then he decides to just let her do her job and enjoy all of the physical contact. Even though she's making the first move, he knows he could still be accused of harassment. He's reluctant to touch her, but he makes a point of not moving out of her way either.

"OK, I just have to reboot the computer and then hopefully the printer will work," she tells him as she starts to sit on his knee. "Oh excuse me," she says, standing back up.

"No, sit down, you deserve to sit after all that work. There's room here," he says pulling her down to share the chair with him.

Darcy A. Cole

As they wait for the computer to boot up, she flirts, "Ok, but don't you think I should get a special reward if what I did fixed the printer?"

"Yes you sure do – what do you have in mind – other than the job, that is?" he flirts back.

"Well yes I would like to be hired as your secretary, but I suppose I'll settle for a big hug for now!"

"OK here's the test, " she says as she hits the button on the printer and they watch the printer begin printing out a test page. She turns around with her arms outstretched ready for her hug, which he eagerly supplies. It's a long tight hug and they both seem reluctant to let it end. Finally, she breaks away. "After all," she tells him, "we have a project deadline to meet and I need to show you I'm a great typist!"

He explains that he still needs to write up the last section of the report, but that she can type what he's already finished writing. He grabs another chair to sit next to her and she starts typing while he's writing. After a couple of minutes, she decides she's thirsty and offers to get them both something to drink.

She comes back into the office looking distressed. "Oh no, you wouldn't believe what happened. I spilled coffee all over my blouse! I rinsed out the stain in the bathroom, but I have to hang it up to dry. You don't mind if I hang it up on this hook so it can dry do you?" she asks as she takes off her top and hangs it up.

"Uh...no...just hang it up there," he says, trying not to stare. He can't believe this is happening. She looks so beautiful. He has to focus on writing the report, but the vision of her typing in just her bra and skirt is almost more than he can take.

He starts to get concerned. What if this is some sort of set-up? What if she's a plant to test his ability to comply with the company's sexual harassment policies? Would they do that? If so, they're making it very hard to resist her. He decides he can't take the risk and needs to ignore her as best as possible. Besides, he figures, test or not he still needs to finish the project by the deadline.

After awhile she stops typing. "I'm all caught up do have any more for me to type?"

Darcy A. Cole

Amazed at how quickly she finished typing the parts he had given her, he responds, "Wow, you sure are a fast typist! I'm not finished writing this section yet. Why don't you take a break while I work on this next part."

"I told you I was good! But you're not paying me to take a break, is there anything else I can do while you're working on that?"

"No, I can't really think of anything. Are you hungry? I'm sure there are some snacks in the coffee room," he offers, thinking that maybe he could concentrate better if she wasn't sitting right next to him, looking so sexy.

She stands up behind him, placing her hands on the back of his neck. "You look awfully tired. How about if I give you a sample of my massage skills and work on this tense neck of yours while you keep writing. Besides, I could hardly go into the coffee room in just my bra! People might wonder what we're doing in here!"

This last statement conjures images of what he wishes they were doing in the office! "Uh, OK, I guess. Yes, that does feel good. I have been very tense."

Seduce Me!

She bends down and whispers in his ear, "Don't let me interrupt. You continue writing while I take care of your physical needs."

Did she just say what I think she said, he wonders, or are my ears hearing things from wishful thinking? Maybe by physical needs she just means my neck. Yeah, that must be it. Yet, he's finding it hard to continue writing as images of her taking care of all of his physical needs keep interfering.

"Doesn't this feel good?"

"Yes, definitely," he responds huskily. He closes his eyes, enjoying the feel of her fingers on his neck.

"Uh-oh, you've stopped writing. I'm going to stop massaging unless you start writing again. After all, you have a deadline and my job is to make sure you meet it as comfortably as possible," she threatens.

"No, don't stop. I can keep writing. See?" he continues. But every time he pauses writing for more than a minute, she stops massaging his neck. He catches on and gets back to writing as soon as she stops massaging.

Darcy A. Cole

"I notice your back is also pretty tense. You lean forward a little so I can massage these muscles, but keep writing or I'll have to quit!"

He complies, of course. After all, he's been killing himself trying to meet this deadline. He deserves some special care, he decides.

This continues for a few minutes, with her massaging and him writing. He's become trained and knows that she'll quit if he pauses writing for too long.

He notices her hands working lower on his back. She must be kneeling behind his chair to reach those lower back muscles...and side muscles, he concludes.

Oh my, those massage strokes are definitely moving further around the sides toward the front of my body. Could her hands be slowly progressing toward my thighs or am I just imagining it? I know one thing, he decides, I will definitely keep writing -- no need to risk her stopping now! He writes for another few minutes.

"Shhh, just keep writing," she responds to his sudden sharp intake of breath after her massaging fingers reached

Seduce Me!

the front of his pants. "I'll keep progressing as long as you keep writing," she whispers.

He can't believe this is happening. Is this a dream? After all, it's been months since he's had a date, not to mention had a woman touch him so provocatively. He keeps writing.

How far does she plan on going, and how am I supposed to ignore *this*, he wonders, as he suddenly hears his zipper being opened! If anyone thinks I'm supposed to make her stop now, he's crazy.

Her hands reach inside. Nah, there's no way this could be a set-up. That settles it, I'm going for it, he decides. I don't know where this will end up, but I know one thing…I'm not going to stop writing now!

Looking back, it was one of the best decisions he'd made in years.

———————————

Darcy A. Cole

6. Being the Best Lover in the World

Being the best lover does *not* require the ability to have sex five times a day, have multiple simultaneous orgasms, or have 60 minutes of intercourse. It doesn't require model-perfect looks or body-builder muscles and you certainly don't have to be young. It doesn't even require knowledge of the latest "expert" techniques.

All it takes to become the best lover is a true desire to understand your partner's needs and a willingness to explore a variety of ways of meeting them.

The best lovers learn how to become in tune with their partner's bodies, interpreting both verbal and non-verbal messages. Their primary goal is to bring their partner

Seduce Me!

complete ecstasy. But sensational sex is not just meant for the enjoyment of one; the best lovers also make sure that they themselves are equally satiated.

The underlying tenet here is that everybody is different. That is, what excites and satisfies one person may not be what does the trick for another. And to complicate matters, what excites and satisfies a person tonight may be very different from what worked last night. That is why just learning the latest techniques is not the answer to becoming a great lover. Great lovers use all of their senses to read their partner's signals, altering their methods as needed.

The Best Lovers in the World

- *Build their partner's self-confidence.* People don't like to do what they don't feel they're good at doing. A good lover finds ways to make his partner feel good about her sexuality. He helps her feel beautiful and sexy, making sure she knows that she excites him. She wouldn't find him staring at or commenting about the bodies of other women and he doesn't allow her to put herself down.

Darcy A. Cole

Good lovers go to great lengths to avoid hurting their partner's ego. He doesn't watch TV during sex and gives his partner his complete undivided attention. He doesn't make her feel silly or perverted for wanting to try something different. Afterwards, a superb lover will point out what his or her partner did that was particularly exciting.

- *Are willing to explore a variety of methods to please their partner.* Excellent lovers take great joy in finding different ways to delight their partner's senses and bring them to higher levels of pleasure. They are curious and open-minded, yet they would never coerce their partner into doing something they are clearly opposed to.

Great lovers are willing to explore a full-range of sexual experiences from sensual to exhilarating sex, from traditional to kinky sex, and from comfortable to adventurous sex. They don't shy away from ideas that their partner introduces, yet will not agree to participate in activities that they have reservations about doing.

Great lovers become aware of their own likes and dislikes, exploring and evaluating the effect of different sensations and delights. They're considerate lovers, willing to give more than they receive, but make sure that they are fully gratified as well.

- **Develop ways to communicate sexual likes and dislikes.** Superb lovers don't think they have to have all the answers and always know the right moves; they understand that what makes them great is their desire to learn about their partner's body and find new ways of pleasuring as time goes on.

Each partner's likes and dislikes can be revealed through verbal or non-verbal communication. Being the best lover means paying attention to your partner's physical reactions (moans, breathing rates, movements) to guide your actions. Great lovers ask their partner to guide them. They also learn how to give their partner clues about their own desires.

- **Learn about their partner's inhibitions and help to release or overcome them.** Shyness, lack of confidence, fear of letting loose, poor body image, conflicting stereotypes, *dis*-empowering beliefs, and poor

---

Darcy A. Cole

experiences are some of the most common factors in preventing sexual enjoyment. As discussed in Chapter 3, professional help may be required in some cases. Regardless, great lovers help their partner fully enjoy the pleasures of making love. They help their partner identify any inhibiting beliefs and then help their partner counteract them through conversation, action, and support.

As we discussed in Chapter 5, couples find seduction scenes to be useful in counteracting some inhibiting beliefs. For example, the role-play where a woman goes to a cosmetic surgeon because she feels self-conscious about the size of her breasts, but instead of operating, the surgeon convinces her that she should not undergo surgery because he finds her body so sexy exactly the way it is, can help counteract her poor body image.

- ***Become masters of seduction by learning what each other needs to become aroused.*** Masters of seduction make it a point to notice things that excite their partners, whether it is an act from a certain movie, or romance novel, or just something witnessed. Anytime she makes a positive remark about an action being romantic, exciting, or special, he makes a mental note.

The best lovers continuously analyze the effect of their actions on their partner. They may even become more knowledgeable than their partner about their partner's turn-ons and turn-offs.

- ***Understand the benefit of anticipation, allowing arousal to peak before seeking and delivering gratification.*** Great lovers don't rush sex, and they don't progress through the stages of arousal too quickly.

When rushed, our internal dialogue goes something like this, "Oh no, don't go there yet, I'm not ready," or, "that was feeling good, why did he quit?" When having nicely paced sex, however, we're often fantasizing about what our partner will do, "I hope he touches me here next," or, "I wonder if she will lick me." The difference in responsiveness to your next move between these two scenarios is immense. The more she desires your next move before you make it, the more she will enjoy it.

How do you know you're partner is ready to move on

Darcy A. Cole

to the next step? Look for physical indications of arousal. As we become aroused, our eyes sparkle, our skin gets flushed, our lips may swell, our pulse quickens, our body temperature rises, our nipples become erect, our breathing gets louder and faster, our bodies begin to move erotically. Does she respond well when you make the next move or does her breathing rate slow? Seduction scenes are excellent ways to slow the tempo and allow arousal to heighten.

- ***Avoid doing or saying anything that has turn-off potential.*** Know the most common turn-offs, but add to the list as you get to know your partner better. When you think of our brains as our most sexual organ, anything that interferes in sexual impulses flowing from our brains throughout our bodies can quickly ruin the ambiance of the moment.

Turn-offs come via any of our five senses. They can disrupt the mood the same way that the sudden bitterness of vinegar would if you had been savoring the sweet taste of warm pudding.

Seduce Me!

The other turn-offs are those that make us feel sexually irrelevant or demeaned. Great lovers make sure that their partner feels valued sexually, in addition to making sure their partner feels valued in non-sexual contexts.

- **Thank their partner.** Thanking their partner is typical of the greatest lovers. Through these two words, much is conveyed. Saying "thank you" implies several positive messages, such as, "I appreciate you," "I relish our love-making," and "your time, attention and sexual actions are gifts and I value every time that you choose to give them to me." Wow, much different effect than, "Hey could you pass me the TV remote?"

Top 25 Turn – offs

Turn-offs are actions that disturb our five senses – sight, smell, sound, touch or taste, or actions that diminish our sexual value. In either case, they interfere with our brain's ability to get or maintain sexual desire. Want to quickly ruin the mood? Try some of these.

1. Poor hygiene (bad breath, dirty nails, body odor)

2. Staring at or ogling other men or women

3. Expecting or demanding sex

4. Grabbing, groping, pinching, biting, sucking too hard

5. Negative comments about a partner's body

6. Efforts to coerce a partner to do something he or she clearly doesn't want to do

7. Faking orgasms

8. Sexual selfishness or self-centeredness

9. Either being critical or taking it personally when a partner wants to have sex, but his or her body isn't responding

10. Getting drunk

11. Withholding sex as punishment or using sex to get something else

12. Expecting to receive oral sex but not give it

13. Assuming that a desire to be hugged or kissed means she wants to have sex

_____

Seduce Me!

14. Runny nose and sniffling

15. Becoming distracted during sex (watching TV, planning your grocery list, answering the phone, etc.)

16. Expecting a partner to automatically know what you want without telling him

17. Progressing too quickly

18. Bad manners (belching, sloppy eating, spitting, etc.)

19. Being less than loving during the day, yet expecting to receive loving at night

20. Comparisons to previous lovers

21. Rough calloused hands

22. Demeaning comments when a partner desires to try something new

23. Insincere obvious gestures designed purely to get sex

24. Wet, sloppy, noisy kisses

25. Unwillingness to practice safe sex

Darcy A. Cole

The *Seduce Me!* process is designed to ignite (or re-ignite) you and your partner's desire for sex. Once fully aroused, partners need to make sure that lovemaking is a satisfying experience for both. The best way to learn methods to satisfy each other is through experimentation and feedback. However, learning different approaches from books and videos can add more variety, give us opportunities to experiment and become better lovers. Use the resources listed in the next section for further information. Enjoy!

Additional Resources

Books

- *Ageless Body, Timeless Mind: The Quantum Alternative to Growing Old* by D. Chopra

- *The Alchemy of Love and Lust* by T. Crenshaw

- *Feeling Good Handbook* by D. Burns

- *Getting The Love You Want: A Guide For Couples* by H. Hendrix

- *G-Spot and other Recent Discoveries About Human Sexuality* by Ladas, Perry & Whipple

- *His Secret Life: Male Sexual Fantasies* by B. Berkowitz

- *How to Give Her Absolute Pleasure: Totally Explicit Techniques Every Woman Wants Her Man to Know* by L. Paget

- *Light Her Fire: How To Ignite Passion And Excitement In The Woman You Love* by E. Kreidman

---

- *Men are from Mars, Women are from Venus* by J. Gray

- *Nice Couples Do: How To Turn Your Secret Dreams Into Sensational Sex* by J. Lloyd

- *Relationship Rescue* by P. McGraw

- *The Romantic's Guide: Hundreds Of Creative Tips For A Lifetime Of Love* by M. Webb

- *Satisfaction: The Art of The Female Orgasm* by K. Cattrall & M. Levinson

- *Total Sex: Men's Fitness Magazine's Complete Guide To Everything Men Need To Know And Want To Know About Sex*

- *Understanding The G-Spot And Female Sexuality: A 10-Step Guide for Unleashing the Ultimate in Female Ecstasy* by D. Hicks

- *What our Mothers Never Told us About Sex* by H. Hutcherson

- *What Women Want Men to Know: The Ultimate Book about Love, Sex, And Relationships for You – And The Man You Love* by B. DeAngelis

---

Websites

- American Medical Association <http://www.AMA-ASSN.org>

- American Association for Marriage and Family Therapy <http://www.AAMFT.org>

- American Association for Sex Educators Counselors and Therapists <http://www.AASECT.org>

- American College of Obstetricians and Gynecologists <http://www.ACOG.org>

- American Psychiatric Association <http://www.PSYCH.org>

- Bippy <http://www.bippy.com/gamesncards.htm>

- Bridal Shower Fun <http://www.bridalshowerfun.com/adultgames.htm>

- Clitical.com - Helping You Hit the Right Spot <http://www.clitical.com>

Seduce Me!

- The Couples Center
  <http://www.couplescenter.com>

- Doctor G – Tools and Education for a Better Sex Life
  <http://www.doctorg.com/index.html>

- Dr. G Spot's Website <http://www.drgspot.net>

- Erotic and Adult Books
  <http://www.booksforwomen.netfirms.com>

- Erotica for Women
  <http://www.eroticaforwomen.com>

- Liberated Christians: The G-Spot and Female
  Ejaculation
  <http://www.libchrist.com/sexed/Gspot.html>

- The Marriage Bed: Sex And Intimacy For Married
  Christians <http://www.themarriagebed.com>

- Network for the Excellence in Women's Sexual Health
  (Drs. Laura and Jennifer Berman)
  <http://www.newshe.com>

Darcy A. Cole

- Physiology of Good Sex
  <http://www.wellness.gatech.edu/sex/physiology.htm>

- Psychological Self-Help by Clayton E. Tucker-Ladd
  <http://mentalhelp.net/psyhelp/chap10/chap10w.htm>

- Sex and Relationships
  <http://www.ivillage.co.uk/relationships/sex>

- Sex Show On Oxygen Cable Channel
  <http://women.aol.oxygen.com/sexshow/> and
  <http://www.talksexwithsue.com/>

- Sinclair Institute (videos and products)
  <http://www.intimacyinstitute.com> or
  <http://www.bettersex.com>

- Society for Human Sexuality
  <http://www.sexuality.org>

Bibliography

AARP. (1999). Modern maturity sexuality survey: Relationships and quality of life factors affecting sexual attitudes, activities, and satisfaction health, sex-enhancing drugs, and sexuality. Washington, D.C.: NFO Research, Inc.

Areton, L. W. (2002, January 15). Factors in the sexual satisfaction of obese women in relationships. *Electronic Journal of Human Sexuality*, Volume 5. Retrieved from <www.ejhs.org>

Barclay, L. (2001, February 14). *Love is all in your head -- or is it in your genes?* WebMD Medical News. Retrieved October 24, 2002 from <http://my.webmd.com/content/article/36/1728_7 2363>

BBC News. (1999, March 10). *Sex keeps you young.* Retrieved October 24, 2002 from <http://news.bbc.co.uk/1/hi/health/294119.stm>

Berkowitz, B. (1997). *His secret life: Male sexual fantasies.* New York: Simon & Schuster.

Betts, K. (2002, March 31). The tyranny of skinny, fashion's insider secret. *New York Times.* Retrieved October 2002 from <http://www.about-face.org/r/press/nyt_033102.html>

Cattrall, K & Levinson, M. (2002). *Satisfaction: The art of the female orgasm.* New York: Warner Books.

CNN.com (1999, February 9). *Sexual dysfunction is widespread in U.S., study says.* Retrieved September 2002 from <http://www.cnn.com/HEALTH/9902/09/sexual.d ysfunction/index.html>

Crenshaw, T.L. (1996). *The alchemy of love and lust.* New York: G. P. Putnam's Sons.

Cyberparent (n.d.) What is chemistry in love relationships?. Retrieved October 24, 2002 from <http://www.cyberparent.com/love/chem1.htm>

DeAngelis, B. (2001). What women want men to know: The ultimate book about love, sex, and relationships for you – and the man you love. New York: Hyperion.

Ellis, B. J., & Symons, D. (1990). Sex differences in sexual fantasy: An evolutionary psychological approach [Abstract]. *Journal of Sex Research,* 27, 490-521. Retrieved 10/24/2002 from <http://www.psyc.canterbury.ac.nz/exp/bruceellis/ Ellis_Symons_1990.html>

Darcy A. Cole

Finestra, C., McEveety, S., & McFadzean, D. (Executive Producers). Meyers, N. (Director). *What women want* [Motion Picture]. United States: Paramount Pictures.

Fisher, H.E. (1992). Anatomy of love: A natural history of mating, marriage, and why we stray. New York: Ballantine.

Harpo Productions (Producer). (2002, June 12). *Oprah* [Television episode]. Chicago: ABC

Hendrix, H. (2001). *Getting the love you want: A guide for couples* (1st Owl Books ed.). New York: Henry Holt and Co, LLC.

Hicks, D.L., (2001). *Understanding the g-spot and female sexuality: A 10-step guide for unleashing the ultimate in female ecstasy.* [E-Book]. New York: Universal Publishers.

Knox, D. (1984). *Human sexuality: The search for understanding.* St. Paul, MN: West Publishing Co.

Kreidman, E. (1990). *Light her fire: How to ignite passion and excitement in the woman you love.* New York: Villard Books

Ladas. A., Perry, J., & Whipple, B. (1982). *The g-spot and other recent discoveries about human sexuality.* New York:

Holt, Rinehart and Winston and New York: Dell
Publishers

Liebowitz, M.R. (1983). *The chemistry of love*. Boston: Little,
Brown.

Lloyd, J.E. (2001). *Nice couples do: How to turn your secret
dreams into sensational sex*. [E-Book]. New York:
Warner Books.

Masters, W.H.& Johnson,V.E. (1966). *Human sexual response*.
Boston: Little, Brown.

McGraw, P. (n.d.). Relationships and sex. *DrPhil.com*.
Retrieved October 2002 from
<http://www.drphil.com/advice/advice.jhtml?conte
ntId=090302_relationships_sexlessmarriage.xml&secti
on=Relationships/Sex&subsectoin=Sexuality>

Men's Fitness Magazine (with Tomkiw, B. & Tomkiw, J.)
(2000). Total sex: Men's fitness magazine complete
guide to everything men need to know and want to
know about sex. New York: HarperPerennial.

Meston, C.M., & Frohlich, P.F. (2000, November). The
neurobiology of sexual function. *Arch Gen Psychiatry*,
vol. 57, Nov 2000. Retrieved November 24, 2002 from
www.archgenpsychiatry.com>

Darcy A. Cole

Midler, B. (n.d.). Retrieved from
    <http://www.brainyquote.com/quotes/quotes/b/q
    130790.html>

Paget, L. (2000). *How to give her absolute pleasure: Totally
    explicit techniques every woman wants her man to know.*
    New York: Broadway Books.

Rako, S. (1996). *The hormone of desire: The truth about sexuality,
    menopause, and testosterone.* New York: Harmony
    Books.

Santamaría, F.C. (1997). *Female ejaculation, myth and reality.*
    Originally presented at 13th World Congress of
    Sexology, Valencia, Spain. Retrieved December 2002
    from
    <http://www.doctorg.com/myth_reality1.htm>

Spink, G. (1996, March). The chemistry of love. *Montage
    News and Views from Monash University* vol.7 no. 1
    [Electronic]. Retrieved October, 24, 2002 from
    <http://www.monash.edu.au/pubs/montage/Mont
    age_96-01/lovedrug.html>

Starr, B. D. & Weiner, M. B. (1982). *The Starr-Weiner report on
    sex and sexuality in the mature years* . New York:
    McGraw-Hill.

Swift, R. (2002). *Satisfaction guaranteed: What women really
    want in bed.* [E-Book]. New York: Warner Books.

Tucker-Ladd, C.E. (1996). *Psychological self-help.* [Electronic].
    Retrieved December 3, 2002 from
    <http://mentalhelp.net/psyhelp/chap10/chap10w.h
    tm>

U.S. Department of Labor Bureau of Labor Statistics. (2002,
    August). National compensation survey:
    Occupational wages in the United States, 2001.
    Retrieved October 2002 from
    <http://www.bls.gov/ncs/home.htm>

Webb, M. (2000). The romantic's guide: Hundreds of creative
    tips for a lifetime of love. New York: Hyperion.

Darcy A. Cole

About the Author

Using her background in health care management, business consulting and writing, the author of *Seduce Me!* explores a topic relevant to all couples involved in long-term relationships: how to rekindle and preserve passion and sexual desire. Specifically, the author employs her considerable experience in researching and aquiring knowledge from state-of-the-art science and adapting it for practical application by relevant populations. Having achieved both failure and success in long-term relationships, she applies scientific research, anecdotal evidence, and personal experience in the development of *Seduce Me! How to Ignite Your Partner's Passion.* The author received her MBA from Northwestern University's Kellogg Graduate School of Management. She welcomes your comments and can be reached via email at: **darcyacole@aol**.com.

If you enjoyed the fully scripted seduction scene in Chapter 5, look for others in the upcoming sequel *Seduce Me! II: More Seduction Scenes to Ignite Your Partner's Passion.*

Seduce Me!

Printed in the United States
1281100001B/289-297